Concept Cars

Concept Cars

An A–Z guide to the world's most fabulous futuristic cars

C H R I S   R E E S

BARNES
&NOBLE
BOOKS
NEW YORK

This edition published by Barnes & Noble, Inc.
by arrangement with Anness Publishing Limited

2000 Barnes & Noble Books

M 10 9 8 7 6 5 4 3

ISBN 0-7607-2168-8

Publisher: Joanna Lorenz
Editorial Manager: Helen Sudell
Editor: Emma Gray
Designer: Alan Marshall
Jacket Designer: Michael Morey
Production Controller: Don Campaniello
Reader: Kate Sillence

Previously published as part of a larger compendium,
The Encyclopedia of Dream Cars

Printed and bound in Singapore

CONTENTS

Introduction

There are few, if any, pieces of hardware as emotive as the car. Through the ages, the car has come to symbolize a love of freedom. The motor car is a means of escape. It can take the driver on a ride to places distant from humdrum, everyday life, and transport the motorist into the future. This is the aim of the concept car – the transformation of dreams into brand-new, ground-breaking designs.

The first concept car was presented in 1939: the Y-job, built by General Motors. Style was as important as practicality and a new role had been created – the car designer. The designer worked hand-in-hand with the engineer, and this powerful combination created exciting new machines that expressed both a vision of the future and advances in engineering technology.

This book is a celebration of these creative, unusual and visually stunning concept cars. We take a look back at what fired the imagination of yesterday's creative minds, and describe the ways in which concept cars have changed over the years. Many of these designs reflect an awareness of the needs of the future. We therefore look at cars that address the problem of traffic congestion, as well as designs that attempt to reduce energy consumption and pollution levels, allowing motorists to live in closer harmony with their natural surroundings. With authoritative text and stunning pictures, this book will guide you through the ideas of the past and hint at the innovations to come.

ALFA ROMEO

■ BELOW *The incredible BAT series was created by Bertone. BAT 5 (left of picture) was unbelievably way-out for 1953, BAT 7 (foreground) was yet more outlandish, while BAT 9 (background) was merely extraordinary.*

Traditionally, Alfa Romeo has aligned itself to the major Italian carrozzieri (design houses) when it comes to design work. It has favoured Bertone, Pininfarina and Zagato, but many other independents have been drawn to the magic that is Alfa Romeo, and Alfa itself has occasionally produced a few of its own dreams in the metal.

Flying saucers and BAT-mobiles

After the Second World War, Alfa Romeo encouraged experimental bodies on its chassis. The Disco Volante ("flying saucer") race cars were a collaboration with Touring, for example, but of all Alfa Romeo's dream cars, the most spectacular were undoubtedly the incredible BAT series – BAT standing for Berlina Aerodinamica Tecnica. All were designed by Franco Scaglione of Bertone. The first in the series of three was the so-called BAT 5, which in 1953 was as way-out as they come. The aim was to create the most aerodynamic shape possible on an Alfa Romeo 1900 chassis, and with a claimed Cd figure of 0.23, it certainly was. The faired-in wings, sideways-popping headlamps and

hawk-like nose were striking enough, but it was the rear-end that got all the attention. Two huge, inward-curving wings rose fantastically around a long central rear "tunnel".

Things got even more outrageous with the BAT 7 prototype of 1954. The rear wings began at the windscreen pillars and became so curved-in that they almost touched each other over the razor-sharp central fin. Huge slots in the

fins equalized side pressure, and an even more aerodynamic Cd figure was claimed. By the time the third and final BAT 9 arrived in 1955, the rear wings had been clipped back to vaguely modest proportions, and there were now side fins from door to tail. After three successive years of making Turin Show crowds swoon, the BAT series was retired. All these cars have since been restored to a glorious condition.

■ LEFT *Ital Design was responsible for the 1969 Iguana prototype, based on the near-racing-specification 33. It was at one point scheduled for a production run but this didn't materialize.*

■ ABOVE *The 1971 Caimano was designed by Giugiaro and featured very angular lines, a flop-forward canopy, pop-up headlamps and an air brake. It was based on the Alfasud.*

■ ABOVE *Ital Design was again responsible for this Alfa Romeo design study called the Scighera. It was intended as an exotic road or racing car.*

■ BELOW *Walter de Silva's masterful hand created the stunning Nuvola, an exercise in a classically inspired sports coupé.*

■ ABOVE *A long bonnet (hood), short tail and classically curved cabin excited public passions.*

Iguana, Spider, Proteo and Nuvola

Ital Design developed another spectacular Alfa concept car, the Iguana prototype of 1969. This was intended to enter production in a small series but it never did. Based on the 33 Stradale mid-engined chassis, it was notable for its brushed-steel body (ten years before the De Lorean) and sharp nose treatment.

■ ABOVE *Simple, stylish and sporty: the Nuvola's wood-and-chrome interior looked both backwards and forwards in time.*

To many eyes the 1994 Spider and GTV production models looked like show cars. To prepare the public for the radical shape of these newcomers, Alfa Romeo designed the Proteo prototype in 1991. This had the rising belt-line and bonnet (hood) cut-outs for the headlamps, which made the Spider/GTV so distinctive, but was based on the 164 and featured four-wheel drive, four-wheel steering and removable glass roof panels.

Alfa Romeo's design boss Walter de Silva was responsible for the striking Nuvola concept car shown at the 1996 Paris Salon. For its inspiration, this handsome car looked back to the great days, not only in its proportion and detailing but also in that it had a separate chassis, in theory allowing any body shape to be designed around it.

Alfa's own shape was extremely elegant: a long, classic bonnet, low, tapering rear, recessed lights and lots of chrome. Despite the retro flavour, it was also ultra-modern: 300bhp aluminium V-six engine, four-wheel drive, six speeds and glorious 18in (45.7cm) alloy wheels. Sadly, despite the precedent set by the Proteo, the Nuvola looked unlikely to become a production model.

BERTONE

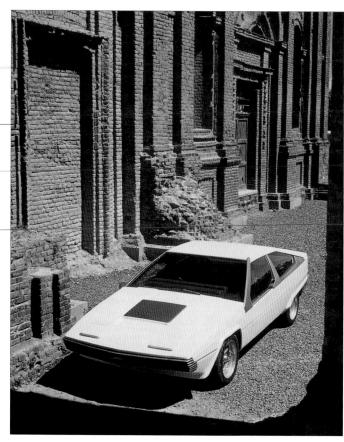

■ ABOVE *Bertone built his Navajo show car on an Alfa Romeo T33 racing chassis, complete with a flat-12 engine. The use of front and rear wings aided downforce.*

■ RIGHT *Along with many others, Bertone must have been disappointed by the styling of Jaguar's XJS. This is his re-interpretation, called the Ascot.*

Rainbow and Athon

Many observers felt that Bertone's Ferrari Dino 308 GT4 was a disappointingly boxy production design. Perhaps to address such criticism, Bertone produced the Rainbow in 1976, based on the mid-engined 308. The name came about because the solid roof could pivot to the vertical and drop down behind the seats, so making the car perfect for rain or sun. The angular lines were uncompromising: there were literally no curves to be seen other than the wheels and exhaust pipes. This model had the distinction of being advertised in the exclusive American Neiman Marcus store catalogue in 1979 but, with a price tag of $200,000, it scared any customers off.

Extending Bertone's reputation for creating pure dream cars, the 1980 Athon was an uncompromising roadster based on the Lamborghini Urraco. It typified Bertone's penchant for bold, squarish shapes joining together to form a whole, themes that would be extended by such cars as the Alfa 6-based Delfino and Citroën BX Group B-based Zabrus.

Bertone's Corvette-based Ramarro won many awards and one designer described it as "representing Bertone's soul". Its hard, geometric shape was emphasized by a completely blacked-out

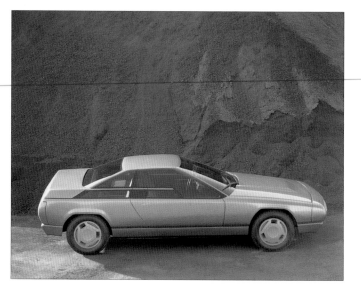

■ ABOVE *The name Rainbow was chosen for this Ferrari-based car because of its potential for use in rain or sun. This show car was unusual in that it was actually offered for sale to special order.*

■ RIGHT *Bertone began taking new dream-car directions with the 1983 Delfino, a three-box coupé based on the Alfa 6.*

■ LEFT *Proteo was the name of this Alfa Romeo Centro Stile prototype. It clearly prefigured the general profile of the later GTV production car.*

■ BELOW *Walter de Silva's masterful hand created the stunning Nuvola, an exercise in a classically inspired sports coupé.*

■ ABOVE *A long bonnet (hood), short tail and classically curved cabin excited public passions.*

■ ABOVE *Ital Design was again responsible for this Alfa Romeo design study called the Scighera. It was intended as an exotic road or racing car.*

Iguana, Spider, Proteo and Nuvola

Ital Design developed another spectacular Alfa concept car, the Iguana prototype of 1969. This was intended to enter production in a small series but it never did. Based on the 33 Stradale mid-engined chassis, it was notable for its brushed-steel body (ten years before the De Lorean) and sharp nose treatment.

■ ABOVE *Simple, stylish and sporty: the Nuvola's wood-and-chrome interior looked both backwards and forwards in time.*

To many eyes the 1994 Spider and GTV production models looked like show cars. To prepare the public for the radical shape of these newcomers, Alfa Romeo designed the Proteo prototype in 1991. This had the rising belt-line and bonnet (hood) cut-outs for the headlamps, which made the Spider/GTV so distinctive, but was based on the 164 and featured four-wheel drive, four-wheel steering and removable glass roof panels.

Alfa Romeo's design boss Walter de Silva was responsible for the striking Nuvola concept car shown at the 1996 Paris Salon. For its inspiration, this handsome car looked back to the great days, not only in its proportion and detailing but also in that it had a separate chassis, in theory allowing any body shape to be designed around it.

Alfa's own shape was extremely elegant: a long, classic bonnet, low, tapering rear, recessed lights and lots of chrome. Despite the retro flavour, it was also ultra-modern: 300bhp aluminium V-six engine, four-wheel drive, six speeds and glorious 18in (45.7cm) alloy wheels. Sadly, despite the precedent set by the Proteo, the Nuvola looked unlikely to become a production model.

AUDI

The Audi name is one of the oldest in the German motor industry, but its post-war career did not begin until Volkswagen bought the Auto Union combine, and the Audi name was revived in 1965. Audi has always been associated with front-wheel drive (and later four-wheel drive) quality saloons (sedans) and coupés.

The brand had just the right qualities for extending the Volkswagen-Audi Group's interests in bold new directions: sportscars, supercars and dream cars, but it was only with the Quattro that Audi finally became a truly aspirational marque.

Quattro Spyder, Avus Quattro

Without a doubt, the Quattro Spyder was the star of the 1991 Frankfurt Motor Show. It also signalled the way ahead for Audi in its exclusive use of aluminium in the bodyshell: this lightweight route would ultimately be used for the A8.

■ BELOW *Undeniably Germanic in form and function, the TT coupé recalled in spirit its ancestors of the 1930s, the great Auto Union racers.*

■ ABOVE *Emphasized by its unpainted finish, the aluminium structure of the Avus was ultra-smooth and lightweight, so that this 6.0-litre V-twelve car was capable of 211mph (339kph).*

■ ABOVE *The Quattro Spyder was a four-wheel-drive mid-engined supercar. Its major significance was the use of aluminium in the bodyshell and a roof-line that inspired a generation of VW/Audi products.*

Equally arresting was the dramatic shape (penned by Erwin Hammel) – all the more so for its bright orange colour scheme. Fitted with a mid-mounted 2.8-litre V-six engine and four-wheel drive, it was claimed to do 155mph (249kph) and reach 60mph (96kph) from rest in less than six seconds.

A mere two months later, at the Tokyo show, Audi upstaged every other concept car with its Avus Quattro, very similar in shape to the previous Spyder but finished in glorious polished aluminium. The quicksilver showstopper recalled the racing heritage of the great Auto Union record-breakers of the 1930s. The specification was breathtaking: a 6.0-litre 60V 12-cylinder engine arranged in three banks of four cylinders and developing 509bhp, four-wheel drive and six speeds. Audi claimed an amazing top speed of 211mph (339kph) and 0-60mph (0–96kph) in just three seconds.

TT and TTS Roadster

The name chosen for Audi's next-generation 1990s sportscars recalled the world's oldest motor race held on public roads, the Isle of Man TT. Destined to become a production model, the TT was first shown as a concept car at the 1995 Frankfurt Motor Show.

■ LEFT *Polished aluminium detailing reflected the use of aluminium in the doors, bonnet (hood), boot (trunk) and engine. Circular dials and red leather trim completed a classy cabin.*

■ BELOW *At the 1995 Tokyo Motor Show Audi presented the TTS roadster, probably even more desirable than the TT coupe. Note the hood (top), held taught like a parachute.*

■ RIGHT *Strong, simple lines epitomized Audi's philosophy of design, while its high performance potential was realized by a turbocharged 210bhp engine.*

A group of young Audi designers created the TT as a car they desired to own, but was accessible to a wide public. Hence, existing Audi technology was used wherever possible: the five-cylinder turbo engine from the A4, and Audi's four-wheel-drive system was used. The 150bhp engine was claimed to produce a very fast top speed of 140mph (225kph).

In style the TT was described as "Germanic" and a vision of the Audi brand. The curves recalled Bauhaus design and pre-war Auto Union racing cars. The show cars' silver paint emphasized the Teutonic element and also betrayed the choice of aluminium for the engine, doors, bonnet and boot (hood and trunk).

The two-plus-two interior was functional and sporting. Traditional sportscar themes were pursued, such as circular dials, leather upholstery, aluminium grab handles supporting the centre console, even exposed rivets securing many metal items. Following quickly on the heels of the TT hatchback coupé show car, at the 1995 Tokyo Motor Show Audi presented the TTS roadster. The most obvious changes were the open top, only two seats, larger wheels and thong-laced leather seats. Under the bonnet, the engine was a more powerful "concept" evolution of the A4 1.8-litre turbo engine, developing no less than 210bhp – good for 149mph (240kph) and 0–60mph (0-100kph) in six seconds.

The most exciting part of the TT/TTS twins story was that Audi planned to put the models into production before the end of the century at a plant in Hungary. This meant that they would be ready to compete with such rivals as the Porsche Boxster and Mercedes-Benz SLK.

■ RIGHT *Both the TTS and its fixed-head TT brother were scheduled to go into production by the end of the century.*

BERTONE

Alongside Pininfarina, Bertone is the greatest design house in the world. Its history stretches back to 1912, when Giovanni Bertone founded a *carrozzeria* in Turin. Bertone's great days began in the 1950s, and it became the first port of call for numerous manufacturers seeking the right design for their new products.

Nuccio and his wicked children

Giovanni's son Giuseppe "Nuccio" Bertone steered the company through its greatest era, boasting a propensity for spotting brilliant young talent: such

great names as Giugiaro, Gandini, Michelotti and Scaglione all served their apprenticeships at Bertone. No one doubts the brilliance of Bertone's production designs such as the Alfa Romeo Giulietta Sprint and Guilia GT or the Lancia Stratos, nor its capacity for manufacturing for Alfa, Fiat, Volvo and others. Bertone also badged several models under its own name, such as the Fiat-engined 850 Coupé, Ritmo Cabriolet and Freelimber off-roader.

The most striking category of Bertone designs were undoubtedly his show cars,

■ ABOVE *Nuccio Bertone was unquestionably one of the most profoundly influential figures in the car world, with a brilliant eye for design talent and an unending capacity to surprise. He died in 1997.*

which he called his "children", and especially those "wicked children", which were controversial or inspired comment. Bertone was rarely interested in practical innovations in his show cars: these were pure dream machines.

Marzal and Carabo

Bertone produced many special bodies in the 1950s on the chassis of Alfa Romeo, Jaguar, Aston Martin and Maserati, but he did not really get into his stride as a producer of dream cars until the late 1960s. One of the most striking of all was the 1967 Lamborghini Marzal, a very novel concept car, which directly inspired the later Espada series production car. Bertone's scheme for a four-seater Lamborghini called for enormous gullwing doors with surfaces almost entirely of glass. This solved the problem of entry to the rear seats and drew attention to the idea. So did the all-silver upholstery!

■ RIGHT *The Marzal was an adventurous step forward in four-seater supercar design. It directly inspired the production of the Lamborghini Espada, although not with the Marzal's glass gullwing doors.*

■ LEFT *The Stratos HF prototype of 1970 was just 33in (84cm) high. The windscreen opened for the passengers to enter, and the steering wheel folded away for easier access.*

■ OPPOSITE *With the Lamborghini Bravo, Bertone experimented with the use of glass as an integrated part of the design.*

■ ABOVE *The Villager was a typical product of the early 1970s fad for beach/ leisure vehicles.*

■ RIGHT *Bertone designed the X1/9 for Fiat, and his own Dallara radical show-car interpretation was intended for racing in the Group 5 class.*

A year later, the Carabo marked another mould-breaking shape: something between a wedge and an arrow. The visual equivalent of a Doppler effect was created by the fluorescent red nose and green tail. The upward-hinging doors anticipated Bertone's Countach by four years, and gave the car its name – Carabo is a contraction of the Italian for "beetle".

Stratos, Bravo and Sibilo

With the 1970 Lancia Stratos show car, Bertone teetered on the edge separating car design from pure sculpture. This amazing machine was designed with a completely free hand and was a car of extremes. It was so low that the driver had to flip up the windscreen and walk in over the front end. To see out, you looked through small windows placed directly behind the front wheels – there was no rear visibility at all. To access the mid-mounted engine, a triangular shape panel hinged upwards like a piano.

The 1974 Lamborghini Bravo (based on the Urraco) integrated elements like the lights, air intakes and rear quarter-lights into the design of the car itself. Another feature was the dark glass, which appeared to form a seamless pane. This theme would be refined with the 1978 Sibilo, an exercise based on the Lancia Stratos. Here the distinction between the metal and glass surfaces was blurred, creating the impression that the body was hewn from a single piece. Inside, the Sibilo's steering wheel was a single solid piece, and the dashboard featured digital instruments set very far back directly in the driver's line of sight.

B E R T O N E

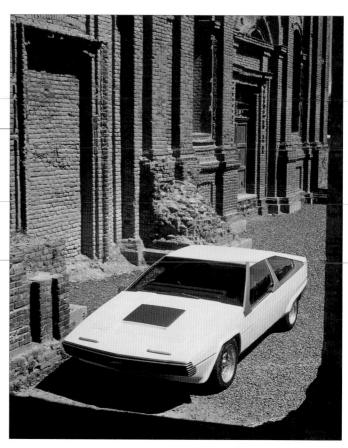

■ ABOVE *Bertone built his Navajo show car on an Alfa Romeo T33 racing chassis, complete with a flat-12 engine. The use of front and rear wings aided downforce.*

■ RIGHT *Along with many others, Bertone must have been disappointed by the styling of Jaguar's XJS. This is his re-interpretation, called the Ascot.*

Rainbow and Athon

Many observers felt that Bertone's Ferrari Dino 308 GT4 was a disappointingly boxy production design. Perhaps to address such criticism, Bertone produced the Rainbow in 1976, based on the mid-engined 308. The name came about because the solid roof could pivot to the vertical and drop down behind the seats, so making the car perfect for rain or sun. The angular

lines were uncompromising: there were literally no curves to be seen other than the wheels and exhaust pipes. This model had the distinction of being advertised in the exclusive American Neiman Marcus store catalogue in 1979 but, with a price tag of $200,000, it scared any customers off.

Extending Bertone's reputation for creating pure dream cars, the 1980 Athon was an uncompromising roadster

based on the Lamborghini Urraco. It typified Bertone's penchant for bold, squarish shapes joining together to form a whole, themes that would be extended by such cars as the Alfa 6-based Delfino and Citroën BX Group B-based Zabrus.

Bertone's Corvette-based Ramarro won many awards and one designer described it as "representing Bertone's soul". Its hard, geometric shape was emphasized by a completely blacked-out

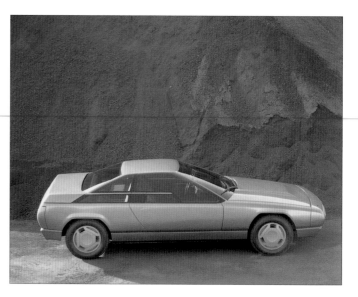

■ ABOVE *The name Rainbow was chosen for this Ferrari-based car because of its potential for use in rain or sun. This show car was unusual in that it was actually offered for sale to special order.*

■ RIGHT *Bertone began taking new dream-car directions with the 1983 Delfino, a three-box coupé based on the Alfa 6.*

■ LEFT *The name Sibilo means "hiss" or "whizz" in Italian, accurately conveying the combined senses of speed and the blurring of the line between metal and glass surfaces.*

■ BELOW *The 1986 Zabrus predicted future shapes like the Alfa Romeo 145. Its basis was the fearsome Group B rally Citroën BX.*

■ ABOVE *Using Chevrolet's Corvette as a basis, the Ramarro was long, low, cleanly finished and sleek.*

■ RIGHT *Bertone's interiors were typically highly sculpted, simple and clean. This is the Athon's exotic cockpit.*

glass top, but not everyone thought the shape had the timeless quality of previous Bertone efforts.

The 1988 Genesis was a people carrier with a difference: it had a 455bhp Lamborghini V-twelve engine mounted between the front passengers. There was space for five people, the rear three sitting in "arrow" formation. Its style and layout were controversial, and the point of having a V-twelve engine was undermined by a long-legged three-speed automatic gearbox.

■ BELOW *The 1980 Athon, based on a Lamborghini Urraco, was a widely admired roadster show car.*

BERTONE

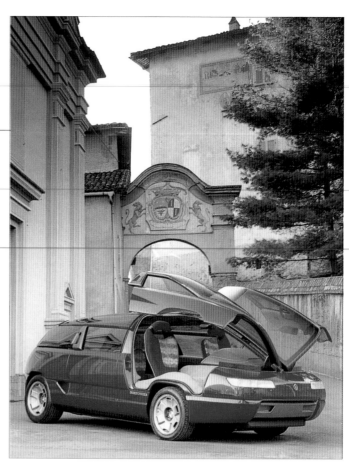

■ ABOVE *Marking a return to the impact of the great show cars of the 1970s, the Nivola used a Corvette ZR1 engine.*

■ RIGHT *"People carriers" were never so radical as Bertone's startling Genesis. The gullwing doors suited its mechanical basis – the Lamborghini Countach V-twelve!*

Nivola, Rush and Blitz

For the Nivola of 1990 (its name recalled the great Italian race driver Tazio Nuvolari), Bertone turned to the Chevrolet Corvette ZR1 for its motive power – and, like all Bertone's show cars, it was a full runner. The bright-yellow concept car featured a targa roof, which stowed above the engine, and hydropneumatic suspension. Most bizarrely of all, it had massaging vibrators in the backs of the seats, claimed to relieve the stress of long

journeys! Perhaps they were needed, for the Nivola measured an expansive 78in (1.98m) wide.

At the 1992 Turin show, Bertone presented two concept ideas. One was part of Fiat's Cinquecento concept display, an outlandish two-seater 4x4 buggy called the Rush. The other was the Blitz electric sportscar. The Blitz was described as a car/bike cross-over.

The sportscar angle was not out of place in an electric car since power response is near-immediate in electric vehicles.

Karisma and Slalom

Despite its rather tacky name, the 1994 Karisma was a fine-looking car based on a Porsche 911 platform. It revived the gullwing four-seater theme pioneered by the 1967 Marzal, and deliberate

■ RIGHT *The exposed front wings and near-tandem seating position echoed Bertone's intent that the Blitz should be a motorcycle/car cross-over.*

■ RIGHT *With its big gullwing doors and four-seat interior, the Porsche-based Karisma was a spiritual successor to the Marzal, seen in the background.*

reference was made to this early Bertone design. The leather-trimmed interior had full seating for four adults, and the gullwing doors were claimed to "allow dignified entry".

A startling shade of orange – said to be inspired by Bertone's favourite champagne, Veuve Clicquot – at least made the 1996 Slalom stand out, not that it needed to with its sports-coupé shape and audaciously designed stacked front and clipped-in rear lights. Adjustable rear seats made the two-plus-two interior fairly practical. Based on the Opel/Vauxhall Calibra Turbo 4x4 floorpan, it was also surprisingly effective to drive.

Nuccio Bertone died in 1997, but left behind him a design and manufacturing empire with the highest reputation, 1500 staff and dozens of clients from around the world. Perhaps his most important characteristic was an ability to spot talent: Marcello Gandini and Giorgetto Giugiaro, the two greatest car designers of recent years, both served as apprentices under Bertone.

■ ABOVE *The orange paintwork of the Opel Calibra-based Slalom was said to be inspired by Nuccio Bertone's favourite champagne.*

■ ABOVE *Rush was the name of this fun-packed, little, two-seater sports off-roader, based on Fiat's tiny Cinquecento.*

■ ABOVE *The Lancia Kayak was undoubtedly more accomplished than Lancia's own later coupé effort, the Kappa.*

CHRYSLER

From Thunderbolt to Turboflite
After GM's Buick had produced the Y-Job, the world's first ever "dream car", in 1939, the first to follow up the idea was its rival Chrysler. Two years later its styling chief Alex Tremulis created the Thunderbolt, a bulbous retractable-top two-door with push-button controls.

After the war, Chrysler collaborated with the Italian design house Ghia to create such dream cars as the Plymouth XX-500 and Chrysler K-310 in 1951. A man called Virgil Exner emerged as the head of styling for Chrysler and directed a whole string of unusually smooth shapes by American standards, notably the Firearrow series of 1953–54, the 1954 De Soto Adventurer and the ill-fated 1956 Norseman, which sunk the Andrea Daria.

The Ghia connection resulted in the striking 1956 Dart, an impressively clean, aerodynamic car (claimed to have one third the drag of conventional cars) with probably the tallest rear fins ever seen. The steel roof was designed to slide back into the rear compartment.

■ ABOVE *Under the tutelage of Virgil Exner, Chrysler produced some extraordinary show cars. This Plymouth Special was seen in the 1957 film,* **Bundle of Joy.**

■ BELOW *By 1965, the first American dream-car golden age was already over, as this tame Plymouth VIP shows. Its main feature was a cantilever roof and rear "office".*

■ LEFT *If you are wondering how you got into the outlandish 1961 Turboflite, when you opened the door, the whole roof and glass lifted up like a clamshell.*

By 1958, Exner's direction had lost its way a little, the Imperial d'Elégance being anything but elegant. The 1961 Dodge Flitewing advanced an interesting solution for a hardtop coupé: the windows opened outwards and upwards automatically on exit. The Turboflite went one better: the whole roof and glasshouse lifted up as one for entry.

Lamborghini revives the dream
Throughout the 1960s Chrysler experimented in the dead-end of turbines, handlebar steering and even

■ LEFT *A liaison with Lamborghini produced the 1987 Portofino, a dramatic mid-engined four-seater with Lamborghini V-eight power.*

■ LEFT *Plymouth's Speedster show car was only 10in (25.5cm) longer than a Mini. It had a mid-mounted 2.0-litre engine.*

■ ABOVE *One of Chrysler's most daring show cars was the Plymouth Slingshot, designed for optimum acceleration.*

vacuum-operated ashtrays. As the years progressed, the dream cars got more predictable; the 1965 Plymouth VIP was typically unadventurous, and Chrysler seemed to have a rude awakening from its dream state.

It took until the 1980s for Chrysler (along with other American manufacturers) to rejoin the dream train and re-establish the American tradition for producing other-worldly machinery.

Perhaps it was Chrysler's purchase of Lamborghini in 1987 that set the ball rolling, although the rise of designer Tom Edle and president Bob Lutz had a huge influence. Certainly its immediate action to create a co-project, which would demonstrate the abilities of the new alliance, produced one of the great show cars of the 1980s. At the Frankfurt Motot Show in the autumn of 1987, the Portofino was displayed. Chrysler described it as the "ultimate mid-engined touring sedan", and most were

inclined to agree. Using a 250bhp Lamborghini Jalpa V-eight engine, this imposing machine featured seating for four, a clamshell bonnet and boot (hood and trunk), and four Countach-style doors, which opened upwards for entry.

The Plymouth Speedster of 1989 was remarkable for its size: at 130in (330cm) long, it was minuscule by American standards, but this marked an attempt to link motorcycle and sportscar themes for the youth market. The result

included a small air deflector, central pop-up headlamps and an interior trimmed in wetsuit rubber.

The wild styling of the 1991 Chrysler 300 show car picked up on Viper themes and catapulted them into the arena of a 17ft-long four-door sports saloon (sedan). Under the long bonnet sat the 8.0-litre V-ten Viper engine, and in front of it was an Allard-style grille. The rear doors were "suicide" (i.e. rear-hinged).

■ RIGHT *Extreme light weight and optimized aerodynamics were behind the Aviat, whose aerospace bias was notable.*

CHRYSLER

■ ABOVE *The name Back Pack suggests outdoor use, and that is precisely what this Plymouth concept car was designed to do.*

■ ABOVE *The double-curvature rear glass of the Thunderbolt was extremely effective. The cab-forward design permitted ample space for four passengers.*

■ RIGHT *Chrysler's portfolio of makes also includes Jeep. This Ecco concept car aimed to take the jeep idea into a more modern fun/sports role.*

Other 1991 show debuts were the Jeep Wagoneer 2000 (a huge estate car (station wagon) with massive 20in (50.8cm) wheels) and the Dodge Neon (a compact saloon (sedan) with sliding doors, fabric roof and a three-cylinder two-stroke engine).

Chrysler increasingly investigated "cab forward" design, and the most extreme expression to date was the 1992 Cirrus; it genuinely did point the way toward Chrysler's future saloon output, although the pillarless construction sadly did not.

From Expresso to Jazz

The 1994 Expresso was a curious taxi-styling exercise described as "Happy Face". Seen from the sides, the windows formed eyes and the bold side accent became a smiling mouth. Making sure you remained happy inside the car was a computer games console and an LCD entertainment module.

Also at the 1994 Detroit show was the Venom, a revival in spirit of the great muscle-car years of the 60s. Its matt-black bonnet (hood), chiselled nose and scooped body sides may have looked evocative but the reality underneath was less intoxicating: it was based around a Neon with a 3.5-litre V-six engine taken from the LH saloon.

Challenging GM's Ultralite in the aerodynamic, low-weight stakes was the

LEFT *Undeniably handsome, the Thunderbolt reflected a new design ethos at Chrysler, the so-called "cab-forward" approach.*

■ RIGHT *This is the 1995 Eagle Jazz show car, whose design traits such as large-diameter wheels and snubbed nose predicted future trends but could not revive the Eagle nameplate.*

Aviat. Looking remarkably similar to the Ultralite, it was claimed to weigh less than 2000lb (900kg) and have a Cd figure of 0.20, thanks to clever ducting at the front and almost jet-plane-style exits in the tail.

For 1995, Chrysler produced a stunning retro-coupé, which owed more than a nod to the 30s Bugatti that shared its name – Atlantic. It was a two-plus-two based around a Viper chassis and was styled by Tom Gale as an expression of the coupé art form. Power

came from two Neon engines joined together to make an eight-cylinder block, with an estimated power output of 325bhp.

Inside, the Atlantic bristled with cushioned leather, rosewood and classical, Swiss-watch-style dials.

When Chrysler's subdivision, Eagle, presented the Jazz at the 1995 Detroit show, pundits instantly recognized this as the future of the model's styling: a bold, snubbed nose, a very long wheelbase and a striking two-piece hatchback tail.

■ ABOVE *For the Atlantic, two Chrysler Neon four-cylinder engines were joined together to make a single 325bhp V-eight with a glorious architectural feel.*

■ RIGHT *The ostentatious Atlantic was made into a proper running car, although, unlike the Viper on which it was based, it looked unlikely to reach production.*

■ RIGHT *The Atlantic was an unashamed throw-back to the design world's glory years of the 1930s. It even shared its name with the car that inspired it, Bugatti's sublime Atlantic coupé.*

CHRYSLER

Pick-ups and concept cars

The Dakota Sidewinder, seen in 1996, reflected an American passion for pick-ups, taking it to the extreme. Chunky, open-topped with a narrow hot-rod-style windshield and a Viper GTS-R 600bhp engine under the bonnet (hood), this was bound to make an impression. The "gas" pedal was marked "Go" and the brake pedal "Whoa"! Perhaps even more outrageous was the Dodge T-Rex, a 6-wheeler based on the Ram pick-up and sporting a 500bhp V-ten engine.

At the opposite extreme. Chrysler presented a China Concept Car, created to satisfy a request from the Chinese

authorities to tender for a new "people's car". The CCC seemed an up-date of the Citroën 2CV, even down to its Bauhaus glass treatment and full fabric roof. Sadly production looked unlikely.

Perhaps Chrysler's most important concept cars for many years appeared at the 1996 Detroit show: the stunningly sleek and sensual LHX and ESX. These were not guts-and-glory sportscars, merely four-door luxury saloons (sedans), but they succeeded in getting everyone excited. The ESX was the more aggressive, despite its diesel/electric hybrid power. The LHX was more traditional and flowing, with a huge

■ LEFT *Imposing in every way, the grand Phaeton measured over 21 ft (5.4m) long and had enormous 22in (55.8cm) aluminium wheels.*

■ BELOW *The Jeep Icon interior had an exposed, paired-down, almost industrial feel to it.*

■ RIGHT *The "dual-cowl-phaeton" style means separate front and rear compart-ments, even two windscreens. The opulence of the rear compartment was unstinted.*

cabin featuring rear-seat airbags and entertainment centre. Its fuss-free, almost pancake-flat shape drew admiring comment from all quarters and some themes appeared in the 1998 model year Concorde/Intrepid production cars.

From Copperhead to Phaeton

A return to sportscars marked the 1997 Detroit show, and the Dodge Copperhead was an exciting 2.7-litre V-six two-seater. It took its name from the Copperhead snake; the dashboard was said to mimic the shape of the snake's head.

Chrysler concepts did not stop there, as it also showed the Pronto small family car, Jeep Icon (the first monocoque Jeep, and very trendy-looking), the Dakar and

■ RIGHT *The Jeep Icon shown in 1997 boasted lightweight unit-body construction, while its youthful looks promised much for the future.*

– probably the most spectacular of all – the Phaeton. This leviathan measured 5.4 metres long and was powered by a 5.4-litre V-twelve engine. It was a modern homage to the great "dual-cowl-phaeton" style typified by the 1940 Newport parade car. The rear passengers had their own windshield, and even their own set of instruments. This was a car conceived to titillate the fancies of a mythical future generation of *concours*

d'élégance devotees, a sad evocation of champagne-glass applause being pushed by Chrysler in its literature.

If there was one thing Chrysler had proved, with its cab-forward revolution and projects like the Viper and Prowler, it was that dream cars need not be confined to an upper stratum strangled by *haute couture* but could genuinely percolate through to the real world, and reach a truly wide public.

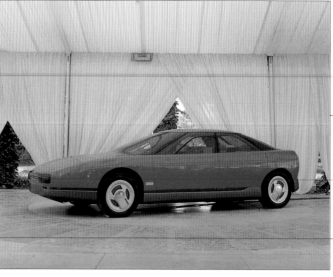

CITROËN

Experiment is the very life-blood of Citroën, as innovations have made their way into its road cars years before other manufacturers come up with similar solutions. One has only to think of the great *Traction-avant* (front-drive) DS, GS, CX and SM to realize how advanced, how individual, was Citroën's technology.

Karin, Xenia and Eole

Falminio Bertoni was the leading light behind Citroën's glory years, but for its birth into the pure dream-car era it appointed a new design chief, Trevor Fiore. His first work was the Karin, presented at the 1980 Paris show. Its pyramid shape was utterly unique, and a reflection of a logical driving position with the driver seated in the middle. This was followed the next year by the Xenia, a rather more conventional hatchback, which nevertheless showed crisp, clean lines.

It was the arrival of American Art Blakeslee that shaped Citroën's real future. Steeped in Peugeot-Simca-

■ LEFT *The Activa was Citroën's 1988 vision of an advanced executive car. Sophisticated technical features were managed suspension, four-wheel drive and four-wheel steering.*

■ RIGHT *Activa 2 was a two-door development of the Activa theme, with a fully active suspension system, which made it into production in the Xantia road car.*

■ BELOW *In 1996, Citroën invited students to design a city car for the 21st century. Norwegian Per Ivar Selvaag's extraordinary proposal was adjudged to convey Citroën's cultural values in a radical package.*

Chrysler values, he began with the ECO 2000, an ultra-economical small car project, and built up to the Eole. Named after Aelos, Greek god of the wind, and Citroën's 1985 exercise was a car designed to cheat the wind. Based on CX components, it was a full four-seater claimed to have a Cd figure of just 0.19, achieved by using flexible body panels, cooling flaps and suspension that lowered as speed increased.

Activa, Citéla and Xanae

The name Activa was used on Citroën's flat-riding Xantia production car, but it first appeared in 1988 on an advanced four-door prototype. This had four-wheel drive and four-wheel steering,

■ BELOW *Although it looked like a three-wheeler, Citroën's 1991 Citéla electric city car prototype in fact had a pair of narrow-set rear wheels.*

■ LEFT *Bertone was responsible for designing the Coupé de Plage, based on the Berlingo van. Its leisure accent is self-evident.*

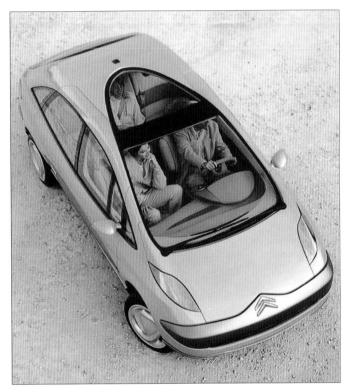

"managed" suspension, highly advanced aerodynamics and a 220bhp V-six engine.

The 1990 Activa 2 was a two-door coupé development of the theme with full active suspension and advanced electronics. However, some industry observers reckoned it looked a little too much like Ford's production line Probe for comfort.

The Citéla of 1991 was an idea for a city electric vehicle, and it was an extremely compact car (just 116in (296cm) long). The rear wheels were set very close together, and the sodium cadmium battery was claimed to last 600,000 miles (966,000km).

Xanae was the name given to a very attractive family car concept vehicle presented at the 1994 Paris Salon. Predicting the way Renault would go with its Scenic, the Xanae was a one-box mini-MPV. It had one door on the left, and two pillarless doors on the right. The quite radical transparent roof was an unbroken continuation of the windscreen.

■ RIGHT *The concept of a compact "people carrier" was given a futuristic slant with the 1994 Xanae. The side doors hinged in opposite directions and the front seats swivelled.*

■ ABOVE *Airflow-style design features included the lights, wing mirrors and a glass roof, which was essentially part of the windscreen.*

DAIHATSU

■ BELOW *A town car, a buggy or a sports/off-roader? Daihatsu let you decide with its Urbanbuggy of 1987.*

Considering its position at the lower end of the Japanese market, Daihatsu has an impressive record of dream and show cars to its credit. These cars go far beyond the self-defined limits of its road-car programme.

Weird dreams

Daihatsu never followed convention. This was proved over and over again by such weird, but fun, concepts as the 1987 Urbanbuggy (an MPV/off-road/buggy cross-over) and the 1985 Trek (a single-seater "box" with a canvas camping-tent top, telephone, TV, spade and winch). With the 1989 Sneaker, a curious little goblin of a car with seating for three, Daihatsu even cast a little bit of magic: the Sneaker lowered a fifth wheel from its rump and rotated itself into tight parking spots.

In 1991, a maturing face was in evidence with the highly appealing X-021, a smooth, retro-styled roadster in the Mazda MX-5 Miata vein. That meant a front-mounted engine (a 1.6- litre 16V 140bhp "four"), rear-wheel drive and an open two-seater cockpit. It was novel in that it had an aluminium space frame, plastic bodywork and race-derived suspension – all expensive items, so it is not surprising that the very pretty X-021 did not make production.

Wacky concepts

Just as impressive was the 1993 Personal Coupé, which, although it was based on humble Charade front-wheel-drive mechanicals, looked neat and was a distinct prospect for production. The same could not be said of the Ultra Mini of the same year, whose main strength was managing to fit four seats into a 98 in- (250cm-) longcar. Its 660cc engine sat under the rear seats. Likewise the Multi Personal 4 was a light-hearted but ultimately daft sports-utility with an interior, which it was claimed was fully washable. Yet another 1993 concept car was the Dash FX21, a very neat electric/ petrol hybrid four-door saloon (sedan).

Daihatsu's crazy Midget III show car of 1995 almost reinvented the Citroën 2CV with its bug-eye headlamps, high roof-line, tiny (659cc) engine and overall charm. Based on a single-seater pick-up, it added rear bodywork and two

■ LEFT *The Midget was a production single-seater pick-up, and the Midget III added a pair of rear seats too.*

■ RIGHT *It was a shame that the handsome X-021 never passed the dream car stage. 140bhp and aluminium/plastic construction sounded enticing.*

rear seats to make a three-seater. Even more ridiculous was the Town Cube, literally a cube on wheels, designed as a joke around the maximum permitted size for Japan's legal class of micro-cars. For the 1997 show round, Daihatsu previewed its vision of a future compact car, the NCX. A capacious, five-seater interior resulted from a long-cabin, short-nose ethic, and the 1.0-litre three-cylinder engine was claimed to produce amazing fuel economy. It proved that, while Daihatsu specialized in small cars, its ideas were actually broad-ranging and consistently forward-looking and experimental.

■ ABOVE *The 1995 Town Cube was really an in-joke: a vehicle designed around the maximum size limits for microcars.*

■ LEFT *Smart, understated and appealing, the 1993 Personal Coupé was a novel idea for a 1.0-litre compact coupé.*

FORD

Perhaps it was Henry Ford's prosaic image as a provider of popular cars that delayed Ford's entry into the dream-car arena. Whatever the reason, Ford lagged behind Chrysler and General Motors in the razzmatazz world of futuristic ideas.

Ford's first dream car

Probably the first true Ford dream car was the X-100 of 1953, which anticipated the torpedo styling themes of later Fords like the 1961 Thunderbird. Another indication of Ford's new directions from the same year was the Mexico – only a scale model, but the result of wind-tunnel testing and an important pointer to future trends. Ford claimed 50 engineering firsts for this car, including a moisture-sensitive cell on the roof, which automatically closed the plastic sliding roof panel.

More extreme was the 1956 Mystere, at once the most amazing and most repulsive of dream cars. Its excessive chromework, double headlamps and heavy body accents appeared in production Fords in years to come, but mercifully the lifting bubble canopy,

swinging steering wheel and gas turbine power did not.

One of the most famous of all 1950s dream cars was the Lincoln Futura of 1955, if only because it was later modified to become the Batmobile in the popular TV series of the 60s. When the double-bubble canopy housed the caped crusaders, its kicked-up tail fins evoked just the right bat-like connotations.

Ford suffers hangover

Ford worked its way through many contorted schools of styling such as the Z-back roof (in the 1957 La Galaxie). It went on to become increasingly unhinged as it proposed a nuclear-powered dream car called the Nucleon in 1958, a gyroscopically controlled two-wheeled car called the Gyron in 1961, a three-wheeled flying car called

■ LEFT
Aerodynamics was one of the obsessions of the 1980s. The Probe IV may have been exceptionally wind-cheating but its wheel spats (skirts) and window cut-outs were utterly impractical in the real world.

■ ABOVE *It took until the 1980s for Ford to come back to the dream-car arena with an aerodynamic two-door concept car called the Probe.*

■ RIGHT *It wasn't realized at the time, but this odd-looking 1981 creation, the aerodynamic Probe III, was basically the forthcoming Ford Sierra. It prepared the public for a radical production shape.*

■ OPPOSITE *Details surrounding this 1956 ⅜ scale model, called X-1000, were extremely vague, like a poorly remembered dream. Ford said the engine could be front or rear mounted, and that the car might even fly!*

■ RIGHT *The name Splash for this 1988 concept car hinted at its capacity to get drenched without getting slushy carpets: the interior was waterproof!*

■ LEFT *The Probe V marked a return to the good old days of gimmickry. The sliding doors and engine cover prove as much.*

Probe and Splash

Future Ford Probe show cars were far more adventurous. The 1983 Probe IV was an amazingly aerodynamic yet practical hatchback. Its Cd figure of 0.15 was spectacular, achieved by wheels covered by urethane "membranes", meticulous airflow management and a spoiler at the base of the windscreen. The ultimate Probe V of a few years later extended the aerodynamic theme still further.

Uniting sportscar and pick-up truck themes was the purpose of the 1988 Splash. Looking like a space-age beach buggy, this striking two-seater had removable windows, roof and rear hatch. Its four-wheel drive, adjustable ride height and retractable mud flaps boosted its chunky off-road flavour, and the colourful weatherproof interior looked trendy enough for its intended youth market.

the Volante the same year and a vast six-wheeler called the Seattle-ite in 1962.

It should not be surprising that, after that lot, Ford's design team and the public had something of a dream-car hangover, and Dearborn's output of show specials petered out in the 1960s.

It took Ford's purchase of the Italian Ghia styling house to kick-start its dream-car programme again in the 1970s. Ghia's creations for Ford (such

as the Coins, Megastar and Action) are described in the pages devoted to Ghia. Ford's domestic US styling studios took longer to return to the dream-world.

Meanwhile, Ford's European subsidiary started a trend of creating show cars that anticipated future production models with the Probe III in 1981. It was all but identical to the Ford Sierra, only the aerodynamic appendages being really different.

■ LEFT *Lincoln's concept car for 1988 was the Machete, whose blade-edged shape perhaps presaged Ford's vaunted "edge-design" school. Note the narrow headlamps.*

■ ABOVE *Inside the Machete, ultra-simple curves combined with digital electronics.*

FORD

■ RIGHT *"Edge design"* was a term Ford used to describe its new corporate design identity. It meant the use of hard-edged surfaces seemingly colliding with one another, and emerged with the GT90 of 1995.

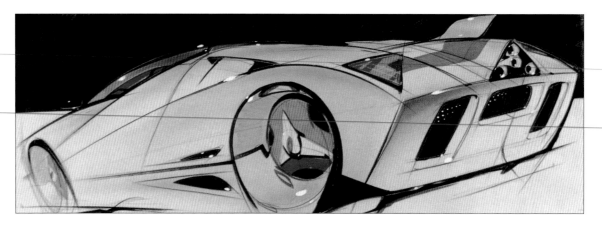

The Contour, shown at the 1991 Detroit Show, was revolutionary in so many respects. Its engine was the first straight-eight since Pontiac's in 1954 and was mounted transversely to save space. The shape of the car was dramatic with steeply raked screens and a long cabin dominating. It was mounted on an aluminium chassis entirely bonded together. The headlamps were 1in- (2.5cm-) high arc discharge rods and there were two floating rear spoilers.

■ LEFT *The GT90's triangular surfaces were most marked from the rear. The large black central triangle is the exhaust outlet.*

■ LEFT *Drawing its inspiration from the GT40 race car of the 1960s, the GT90 it was a very low, rakish, mid-engined supercar.*

■ ABOVE *Ford's designers applied "edge design" to a road-going IndyCar-inspired concept car called the IndiGo.*

■ ABOVE *A black front spoiler and wings created a race-car feel on the outside, while the hi-tech construction and sequential six-speed gearbox did so under the skin.*

Edge design

To describe its fresh way of thinking in design terms, Ford coined the term "edge design". Before production cars like the Ka and Puma took to the streets, Ford displayed numerous concept cars at motor shows around the world, which dramatically demonstrated its new philosophy.

Edge design burst on to the scene with the revolutionary GT90 in 1995. The name hinted at the inspiration for the car, Ford's highly successful GT40 road/race car of the 1960s. In format, there were similarities: this was a very low, mid-engined two-seater with fantastic performance potential, but in truth the cars were very divergent.

The GT90 resembled a Stealth bomber in the way that its triangular flat surfaces intersected one another. Under the skin, its technology was bang up-to-date racing-car: a honeycomb aluminium chassis, carbonfibre body and space-shuttle-type ceramic exhaust. Powered by a quad-turbo 720bhp V-twelve engine, it was intended to be launched in a limited series of 100 cars, but the plan never materialized. Much more significant was the GT90's effect on the future of Ford design.

IndiGo racer

It was not just the name of the IndiGo that was clever (playing on its association with IndyCar racing). This was no mere show car but a concept designed from the outset to be feasibly manufactured at some point. Even though most people who worked in the trade accepted that this was too radical to be offered for sale, it was a driveable car.

Ford said that the IndiGo "captures the essence of the race-track and transforms it into a realistic design for the street". The styling was strongly race car in feel, from the bespoilered, narrow nose to the blacked-out wings, while its construction (carbonfibre, aluminium and glassfibre) also mimicked competition use.

A 441bhp 6.0-litre V-twelve engine – formed by mating two V-six units together – was estimated to give a top speed of 170mph (273kph) and a 0–60mph (0-96kph) time of under four seconds. The six-speed sequential gearbox was derived from race cars, and changes were made by pressing buttons on the steering wheel. Even the instrument panel on the dashboard was Formula 1 inspired.

■ LEFT *In the centre of the car was a six-litre V-twelve engine with 441bhp at its disposal.*

FORD

Lincoln, meanwhile, forged ahead with its own L2K concept (in 1995), a possible future competition for the Mercedes-Benz SLK. Its blade-like shape (created by an affiliated design house called Concept Car Company) hid a 250bhp 3.4-litre V-eight engine. The following year came the Sentinel, a

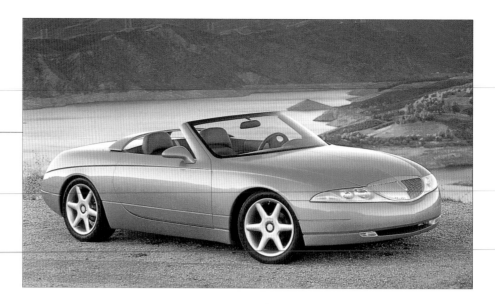

■ ABOVE *Lincoln's L2K concept car was a V-eight front-engined roadster, pitching Lincoln into an area it had not explored before.*

■ LEFT *With a different set of wheels, the L2K was able to do the rounds of the show circuit with a dash of novelty.*

startling expression of Ford's edge design ethos: a high waistline, wonderfully sculpted lighting, ultra-clean, flat shapes and elegant proportions. It was a huge car, but felt right, and was even made into a runner on a lengthened Jaguar platform.

■ ABOVE *A very high waistline, clean shapes and good proportions made the Sentinel one of the most striking concept cars of 1995.*

■ LEFT *One of the most extreme expressions of "edge-design", if not the most elegant, was the Lincoln Sentinel.*

■ ABOVE *Computer animation and advanced voice-activated controls made the Synergy 2010's interior appear vastly different from today's cars.*

■ ABOVE *Synergy 2010 was an extremely bold styling statement, projecting ideas for a family car for the year 2010.*

The Synergy 2010 was Ford's idea of a family car for the year 2010, presented in 1996. As such, it featured two power sources – a 1.0-litre direct-injection engine feeding an electric motor – extremely lightweight materials (it weighed just one tonne (ton)), "air fences", which dictated the car's advanced, aerodynamic styling and voice-activated controls matched by computer-animated instruments. You could even call up   the phone book by issuing a simple verbal command!

Just as the Ghia Saetta broke the path for the radical new Ka, so the 1996 Lynx dropped a few clues about the forthcoming Fiesta-based Puma coupé. One element that was lost in production was the odd twin roll-bar layout, which also formed the side window frames and guides for a fold-away roof.

Mercury's 1997 MC4 extended edge design to a mid-market four-seater. It looked good but still incorporated such dream themes as miniature "suicide" rear doors and a gullwing boot (trunk). More exciting still was the MC2 concept car shown at the 1997 Frankfurt Motor Show, in essence a new Ford Cougar. Here was the most successful and satisfying expression of edge design yet, a powerful combination of good proportions, aggressive angles and a lean profile.

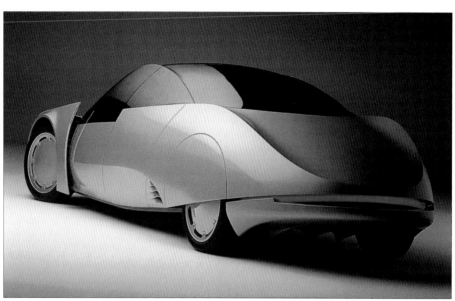

■ ABOVE *Extremely light weight and aerodynamic, the Synergy 2010 used a petrol/electric hybrid propulsion system.*

■ BELOW *Shown at the 1997 Frankfurt Motor Show, the Mercury MC2 was perhaps the most elegant "edge design" concept yet from Ford.*

GENERAL MOTORS

More than any other car-maker in the world, General Motors has embraced the dream-car theme with a vengeance. It was arguably the creator of the world's first dream car in the sense of a car created purely for advancing ideas rather than production realities: the Buick Y-Job of 1939 was a world pioneer. It had long, sleek lines, concealed headlamps and an electric top, which hid under a metal cover when lowered. The dream car had been born.

Harley Earl and Motorama

From then on, General Motors was the spiritual home of the dream car. The architect of this style revolution was Harley Earl, and it was his 1951 Buick Le Sabre that launched the jet-plane era

■ LEFT *One of the stars of GM's Motorama road shows of the 1950s was the Pontiac Club de Mer. This blue-anodized aluminium roadster was just 38in (96.5cm) high.*

of car design in America. Not only did it look fantastic, it bristled with innovation: cast-magnesium panels, a hood (top) that raised itself automatically when a sensor detected rain and heated

■ BELOW *The 1954 Buick Wildcat II had a glassfibre body. Note the "leaping-cat" bonnet mascot (hood ornament) and headlamps mounted by the windscreen.*

seats. The Buick XP-300 of the same year was also ahead, with sleek styling, locking side-impact bars, hydraulic seats and a methanol-powered engine.

Throughout the 1950s, GM laid on the flash, brash razzmattazz in giant mobile shows called Motoramas. The centre-pieces of these showy extravaganzas were always the latest creations of stylists obsessed with futuristic visions of a brighter, faster, bigger age. In the peak Motorama year (1956), GM spent £6 million ($10 million) on the shows and attracted two million spectators.

By then Harley Earl was the General's styling supremo. It was he who introduced the very idea of "style" into everyday motoring and the yearly changes of model, which are pursued in America to this day. Earl liked to introduce "concepts" at Motoramas, which might one day reach production. Some did, like the Corvette and Cadillac Eldorado Brougham, but most were, of course, far too way-out.

Firebirds and the Bonneville Special

These were the crowd-pleasers. The public swooned at the sight of cars like the Buick Le Sabre and XP-300. Most drastic of all, the XP-21 Firebird of

■ BELOW *Jet turbine styling and some genuine jet-fighter components gave the Pontiac Bonneville Special a science fiction spin.*

■ ABOVE *The 1956 Oldsmobile Golden Rocket featured roof sections that folded upwards when the door opened, while the seats swivelled and the steering wheel split in two to aid access.*

■ BELOW *Firebird II toned down the fighter plane extremes of the XP-21 in a body that could seat four people. Fins, turbines, a bubble roof and titanium bodywork kept the razzmatazz going.*

■ ABOVE *Nominally a feasibility study to ascertain the viability of gas turbine power, the XP-21 Firebird was essentially a shock publicity exercise.*

1954 was utterly sci-fi, its small jet-plane turbine propulsion being taken to extremes with a jet-fighter-style body: if you took away the wheels it really looked like a single-seater plane.

The Firebird evolved through two further generations. The Firebird II of 1956 had a central joystick and was claimed to have overcome the heat and noise-generation problems of a jet turbine engine. The more down-to-earth bodywork was in titanium, while passengers entered through a transparent canopy. The 1958 Firebird III returned to moon-rocket influences, sprouting aero-fins all over and boasting double bubble tops, a central lever for steering/braking/acceleration, cruise control, remote door-opening and "electroluminescent" instruments.

One of the best 50s dream cars was the 1954 Pontiac Bonneville Special. This was Earl's idea of a dreamy sportscar, full of glitz like fat chrome bonnet (hood) strips, chrome-mustachioed gaping grill, wrap-around screens, gullwing bubble-top and aircraft-style interior. It was the rear-end that was best, however: a Continental-style spare wheel cover with a turbine trim, flanked by jet-style tail lights.

■ LEFT *Sci-fi met hi-tech in the Firebird III. Beneath the huge fins lay pioneering electronic controls. There was even provision for the car to drive itself via cables mounted under GM test tracks.*

GENERAL MOTORS

General Motors' output was prolific. In just one year (1954) no less than 12 different dream cars were paraded in front of the public. This was the golden age of the dream car, and GM was its golden child. GM stuck to "style" and "innovation" less than the outlandish themes of other US names, and often its show car ideas would become production realities.

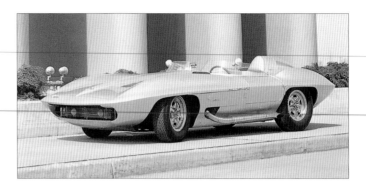

■ LEFT *GM styling supremo Bill Mitchell built the Sting Ray as early as 1959 as his own personal car. It inspired the later Corvette Sting Ray production car.*

■ BELOW *In 1962, the Mako Shark evolved from the Sting Ray. It was Corvette-based, and took shark-like styling themes to their conclusion.*

Rocket, Shark and Stingray Roadster

Highlights of the 1950s included the Buick Centurion, the remarkably clean Oldsmobile Golden Rocket, the 38in- (96.5cm-) high Pontiac Club de Mer, the 1957 Chevrolet Corvette SS (reminiscent of Jaguar's D-Type in many ways), and the jet-style Cadillac Cyclone.

General Motors lost none of its touch in the 1960s. Stylist Bill Mitchell drew inspiration from sharks in his 1962 Corvette Shark study: inlets for gills, exhaust pipes for fins, a pronounced snout and a graduated blue colour scheme. This followed the design of his own personal car, the Sting Ray Roadster, which also did the show rounds.

■ ABOVE *A paragon for suburban shopping bliss: the Runabout's front wheel could turn through 180 degrees to ease parking, while the tail contained two detachable shopping trolleys (carts)!*

■ ABOVE *To get into the 1967 Chevrolet Astro I, you popped a switch and the roof rose up, carrying the seats with it. It looked spectacular but was plainly a crazy idea.*

■ RIGHT *By the 1970s, the Golden Age of dream cars was over. In 1973, Bill Mitchell created this Pontiac Phantom show car as a swansong.*

Similar themes persisted in the 1963 Corvair Monza prototypes, transforming the beleaguered rear-engine Corvair into lithe sportscars, which undoubtedly influenced the next generation of sports shapes.

From Runabout to Aerotech

GM pursued other ideas too. Its Runabout was a vision of tomorrow's shopping car, a three-wheeler with two removable shopping trolleys (carts) built into the rear. The XP511 was a hybrid commuter trike with a huge clamshell canopy, and the Astro I incorporated a novel system of entry: the whole rear bodywork raised upwards, lifting the two seats with it.

Unlike the other US car manufacturers, GM never gave up its show car programme, pursuing dream themes into the 1970s with projects like the quad-rotor Chevrolet Aerovette and Pontiac Phantom.

The next major GM activity occurred from the mid-1980s on. GM concentrated on exceptionally exotic supercar projects like the Buick Wildcat of 1985, the Corvette Indy, the Pontiac Pursuit and, possibly the most extreme of all, the Oldsmobile Aerotech, with an amazing top speed in excess of 250mph (400kph).

■ LEFT *General Motors returned to the dream-car arena with a bang in 1985: the Buick Wildcat revived a famous dream-car name and catapulted it into the present day.*

Cadillac pursued a theme of luxury express transport. Following the 1988 Voyage, the more accomplished Solitaire of the following year was "one of the world's most aerodynamic vehicles" with a Cd of 0.28, the result of such wind-cheating additions as wheel spats (skirts) and faired-in headlamps. It was powered by a 6.6-litre V-twelve engine developed by GM and Lotus and featured electronic articulated doors.

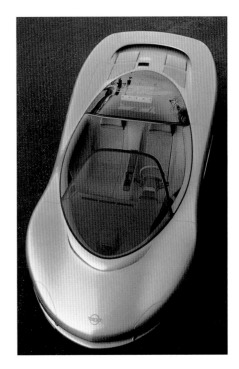

■ RIGHT *In 1986-87, the Oldsmobile Aerotech broke new world speed records: the short-tail car reached 257mph (414 kph), the long-tail an incredible 278mph (447 kph). And all from a 2.0-litre engine...*

■ ABOVE *The 1986 Corvette Indy concept car judged the spirit of the times to perfection, as an all-out mid-engined supercar of prodigious performance.*

GENERAL MOTORS

Stinger, Sunfire and Camaro

In 1989 came the Pontiac Stinger, an aggressively styled sports-utility vehicle. Adaptability was the name of the game here: all of its carbonfibre panels could be removed, as could the glass roof and the lower glass door panels (which could be replaced by a cool box and storage unit). Inside, four seats were adjustable six ways, while the rear passengers could elevate themselves by 15in (38cm) for a grandstand view over the roll-bar. Also

■ ABOVE *Impressive aerodynamism and a V-twelve experimental engine made the Cadillac Solitaire a limousine for dreamers. The Voyage is in the foreground.*

■ BELOW *Chevrolet's California Camaro was a vision of the future direction of GM's successful Camaro series.*

■ ABOVE *Pontiac's Sunfire was GM's expression of the cab-forward style espoused by Chrysler. The rear doors hinged from the back.*

supplied were a compass, phone, vacuum cleaner, stove, picnic table, umbrella and dustpan!

Pontiac's 1990 two-litre turbocharged Sunfire concept stole a page from Chrysler's cab-forward school of design in a two-plus-two coupé shape. One unusual feature was a set of "suicide" doors for the rear occupants, an idea dropped two decades earlier by every car-maker. The main point of interest, however, was the instrument binnacle: it was located in the centre of the steering wheel but was mounted to remain upright whichever way the steering wheel was turned.

The Camaro was always a badge that GM liked interpreting for the future. The California Camaro was typical: a far-sighted "running sketch in metal". A flamboyant use of glass, gullwing doors

■ LEFT *Impact was the name GM gave to its initial prototype for an electric sportscar. It actually entered production in little modified form as the EV1.*

■ BELOW *The Ultralite showed GM was thinking in many directions. Thanks to extreme light weight and smooth airflow, the Ultralite could reach 135mph (217kph) yet return up to 100mpg (160kpg).*

and a sharp-nosed treatment were notable features, while such fripperies as a vacuum cleaner in the console undermined its seriousness.

Experimental and Rageous

Chevrolet's CERV (Corporate Experimental Research Vehicle) projects stretched from the cigar-shaped 1960 single-seater to the 1990 CERV III, which built on the 1986 Corvette Indy. The CERV III was created with assistance from GM's newly acquired Lotus wing and used a heavily modified Corvette ZR1 engine producing no less than 650bhp, mounted centrally. Drive was to all four wheels through an automatic gearbox with six speeds, and the top speed was quoted as 186mph (299kph), with 0–60mph (0-96kph) coming up in 4.2 seconds. Active suspension, carbonfibre brakes and a Cd figure of just 0.274 were also

something GM wanted to shout about.

For the 1992 Ultralite, the claims were different: 100mpg (160kmp) economy and a top speed of 135mph (217kph). This was possible thanks to a carbonfibre body weighing just 420lb (190kg) and a Cd figure of 0.192. Yet it could still fit four adults.

The Sting Ray III (also 1992) pointed a little toward a new Corvette, with its longer wheelbase and shorter length.

Some regarded this concept car as superior to the C5 Corvette of 1997.

GM pioneered the productionization of a ground-up electric vehicle: the EV1 was launched in 1996. It all started life as the Impact concept car, an innovative and very sleek (Cd 0.19) coupé. Unlike any other electric car then developed, the Impact was a performance car, capable of accelerating to 0–60mph (0-96kph) from a standing start in under nine seconds. Its bonded aluminium spaceframe and composite body helped in keeping overall weight down.

With its Rageous concept car (1997), GM's Pontiac division created a Batman-style car described as a "sports coupé with the practicality of a sports-utility". Clearly an answer to Ford's edge-design thinking, it was a striking but not entirely happy mix of bold, folded edges and colliding shapes. Space inside was far better than in most sports coupés.

■ LEFT *General Motors built this Sunraycer solar-powered car to compete in long-distance sun-propelled competitions.*

GHIA

It is perhaps a sad reflection that to most people Ghia means a trim-level badge on their humdrum Ford. That all stems from Ghia's 1973 acquisition by Ford, but its history as one of the most illustrious Italian design houses stretches back to the early years of the 20th century. Ghia's main business was creating bespoke (dedicated) coachwork for high-quality Italian chassis, in which

■ ABOVE *Virgil Exner was responsible for the extraordinary Selene II. The driver sat alone in a central position, while the passengers faced backwards and had a TV screen to watch!*

■ ABOVE *The 1959 Selene was a sleek, nose-heavy "people carrier" styled by Tom Tjaarda. This forward-control style was advanced by several designers, but its dynamic shortcomings consigned it to an early grave.*

it was extremely successful. These were the original dream cars – one-offs built for wealthy clients, certainly not "show cars" in the accepted sense.

In 1950, Chrysler sent a Plymouth chassis to Turin, and Ghia rebodied it to become the XX-500. Although it looked ponderous, it sparked an association that led to Ghia building many of Chrysler's 50s dream cars. Ghia got into its stride with some stunning coachwork, and the 1953 Fiat 1100 Abarth and Fiat 8V were trend-setting.

Aerodynamics and style

Undoubtedly, the 1955 Ghia Streamline (or Gilda) was one of the most spectacular shapes of the 1950s. Created in a wind tunnel at Turin Polytechnic, this long, radically finned

device mutated through several generations, still being displayed at shows with great succes as late as 1960. Aerodynamics were a Ghia speciality, as proven by the Nibbio record breaker, which reached 100mph (161kph) on

350cc. Ghia also made the beach-car milieu its own with a string of wicker-seated Fiats called Jolly, and manufactured its own range of sportscars with the Dual-Ghia Firebomb, L6.4, 450/SS and 1500.

■ LEFT *At the 1961 Geneva Motor Show, Tom Tjaarda's IXG dragster was displayed. However, it was too streamlined to accept its intended Innocenti engine.*

■ OPPOSITE *The 1955 Turin show, where the world was enraptured by Ghia's incredible Streamline/Gilda, which boasted the largest tail fins of the era.*

■ RIGHT *The 1974 Coins was a vision of a future Ford Capri, although its bulbous styling (by Tom Tjaarda), three-abreast seating and single hatchback door for entry represented gimmickry, not advancement.*

A very talented man called Tom Tjaarda became one of Ghia's main stylists, and he made a big impression with the 1959 Selene, a sort of super-sleek forward-control "people carrier". Its follow-up, the Selene II of 1962, had a central driving seat and two rear seats facing backwards.

Then another brilliant stylist called Giorgetto Giugiaro joined Ghia from Bertone and designed many exceptional production cars. He also penned some attractive Ghia show cars, such as the Maserati Simun, the De Tomaso Pampero and the Oldsmobile Toronado Thor.

After its acquisition by Ford Ghia in 1973, Ghia was used as the European styling and prototype wing of Ford's global organization. Immediately, Ghia came up with a string of concept cars, inevitably based on Fords. Early examples were the Mustela (a Capri

alternative), the Tuareg (an off-road Fiesta) and the Microsport (a truncated Fiesta-based sports coupé).

Radical wedges

Its best designs in the 1970s were also its most radical. The 1974 Coins was a striking curved wedge with a single rear-sited door. The 1977 Megastar was a Granada-based saloon (sedan), though you

would never guess so from its amazing glass-house moulding (the front doors were 80 per cent glass). The Corrida was a chunky little safety-orientated sports coupé.

Probably the most striking Ghia show car of all was the 1978 Action, the most severe wedge shape ever seen. Designed by Filippo Sapino, it had a rear-mounted DFV Formula 1 V-eight engine and completely enclosed rear wheels.

■ LEFT *The Corrida was a pretty 1976 gullwing show car based on a Fiesta floorpan.*

■ BELOW *In 1977, Ghia showed the Megastar, a four-seater with a very swoopy glass waistline, based on Ford Granada parts.*

■ ABOVE *This car's name – Action – says it all. Styled by Filippo Sapino, its uncompromising wedge shape was highly dramatic for 1978, as was its Formula 1 power plant.*

GHIA

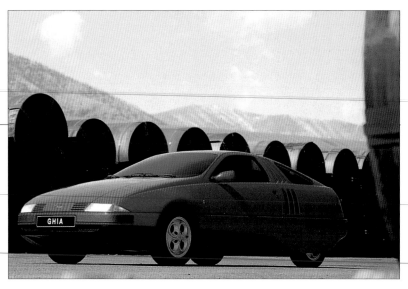

■ LEFT *Based on the Ford Granada, the Altair was a very successful design exercise.*

■ ABOVE *One of Ghia's most attractive concept cars was the Escort XR3-based Brezza. Its engine was mid-mounted.*

In the 1980s, Ghia continued as a prestige *carrozzeria*. Its Granada Altair project was dignified in its simplicity, while the Avant Garde and, in particular, the Brezza (both Escort-based) were delightful compact coupés. Ghia also produced an attractive body for the mid-engined AC ME3000.

A host of microcars followed: the five-seater but small Pockar, the Shuttler, the three-wheeled Cockpit and the Trio. It was a shame to many that more was not made of the Barchetta, a Fiesta XR2-based roadster, which might have been a

■ RIGHT *Ghia even flirted with the idea of a tandem two-seater three-wheeler called the Cockpit. The whole glass roof lifted up for access.*

■ BELOW *The British sportscar firm AC had connections with Ford, and this handsome 1981 Ghia reworking of its ME3000 sports car was once destined for production.*

modern Ford-badged answer to the MG Midget. Less successful was the seven-seater APV, a car which the then UK Prime Minister, Margaret Thatcher, famously wanted to be redesigned.

Via, Zig/Zag and Connecta

Much comment was attracted by the 1988 Saguaro, which predicted the softer, rounder styles of the 1990s in a sporty, four-door package. The 1989 Geneva showing was the Via, a "Ford Sierra Cosworth for the next decade". Designed by a team of British stylists – brothers Ian and Moray Callum, David Wilkie and Sally Wilson – it was a very smart and sleek four-door saloon with an intended specification that included a turbo V-eight engine and six-speed

■ ABOVE *Perhaps the Barchetta represented a missed opportunity, for this could easily have been a compact Ford roadster ahead of its time.*

■ ABOVE *The Zig and Zag were a jocular pair of extremely compact youth-oriented show cars. Zig was the sportscar, Zag the van.*

gearbox. One of its highlights was a fibre-optics system for navigating in fog; another was a fully detachable photo-sensitive glass roof.

An interesting pair of leisure cars was created for the 1990 Geneva Motor Show, both based on a cut-down Fiesta platform. The Zig was the more engaging of the Zig/Zag pair (the Zag was a van). Designed by David Wilkie, the Zig had a very short bonnet (hood) flanked by pinhole headlamps and a perspex (clear plastic)-shrouded cockpit. The Sally Wilson-designed interior was strikingly finished with dashboard instruments painted blue, green and orange and a rear-view mirror that sprouted, tentacle-like, from the facia.

■ ABOVE *The 1989 Ghia Via was a high-performance four-door saloon (sedan) with V-eight power and super-sleek styling.*

■ ABOVE *Ghia went microcar-mad in the 1980s with a whole string of city car projects. This one is called the Trio, because three people could be seated in it.*

■ RIGHT *Saguaro was the name of this 1988 sporty four-door, which predated shapes like the Renault Mégane by a decade.*

GHIA

■ ABOVE *The extremely lightweight Connecta marked a new direction for Ghia – electric power.*

■ RIGHT *Ghia styled this Lagonda Vignale-badged show car for Aston Martin. It revived the Vignale name-plate – Ghia having taken over coachbuilders Vignale in 1969.*

Having an Escort van as a basis might not sound very exciting, but Ghia's 1992 Connecta was an important show car: it was Ford's first electric show car. The body-shell was in lightweight carbon-fibre and could seat six people (four forward-facing, two rearward) in a length of only 166in (421cm).

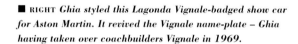

■ ABOVE *The Alpe was Ghia's vision for a competitor in the burgeoning sports-utility market sector.*

Focus and Lagonda Vignale

One of the most radical and adventurous dream cars ever was the Ghia Focus, presented at the 1992 Turin show. Based on a shortened Ford Escort Cosworth platform, it was naturally a very rapid sportscar. But it was Taru Lahti's styling that made the biggest impression. Novel features included whale-like front stabilizers, interesting headlamp architecture, distinctive air intakes,

alien-like grab handles down the body sides, scalloped rear fins, central rear-exit exhaust and amazing "bubble" rear lights. The cabin was equally avant garde, combining organic shapes and natural materials with an exposed, stark treatment and curious, off-centre detailing. The Focus might have made production as a Ford but was judged too radical and too expensive.

Of the Lagonda Vignale shown at the 1993 Geneva show, much was said and even more expected, for this might have made a future four-door Aston Martin (Ghia and Aston were now owned by Ford). Moray Callum designed the Lagonda Vignale, which was variously described as "trend-setting", "marvellous" and "the ugliest car around" – it all depended on your viewpoint. There was certainly nothing retiring about this substantial saloon (sedan), least of all the grille, the high waistline, huge wheels and drooping tail.

Ford's design dynamo

Ghia cemented its reputation as Ford's think-tank with two concept cars launched at the 1996 Turin show. One

■ ABOVE *One of the most radically styled of all Ghia show cars was the 1992 Focus, which stood a strong chance of entering production. Note the intriguing side "rails".*

■ RIGHT *Based on an Escort Cosworth floorpan, the Focus was extremely accomplished in action. Note the curious "bubble" rear lamps.*

was a clear signal of how the forthcoming Ford Ka would look: the radical Saetta's front end was shared with the Ka. In other respects, it was wildly different, Ford's prevailing edge-design mentality being taken to the limit. Dominated by a central roof rib, the silver-and-blue concept was bold in its geometric shapes, especially the rear lights. The other Turin debutant was the Alpe sports-utility, based on the Escort, with chunky, solid styling and a hint of off-road ability.

Today, Ghia's role is less as a creator of dream cars and more as a design dynamo in Ford's global empire, and a useful prototype-building facility in Italy's car design heartland. The Ghia badge persists on Ford products as an indicator of the highest level in its car ranges, but it is perhaps more fitting to remember the great legacy of the Ghia name by its impressive back catalogue of striking and innovative car designs. If only Ford had the courage to produce such brilliant creations as the Focus, the motoring world would be a better place.

■ LEFT *The gauges reflected the Focus's forward-thinking yet classically inspired form. Organic forms melded with stylized detailing.*

■ BELOW *The 1996 Saetta fitted in with Ford's "edge-design" mentality, and prepared the public in for the radical small Ka.*

HONDA

Traditionally, Honda always shied away from producing concept cars, presumably because it viewed its mainstream cars as advanced.

Biting the dream-car bullet

Finally in 1991, Honda bit the dream-car bullet when it displayed a pair of models at Frankfurt.

These were the FS-X saloon and EP-X coupé. The FS-X (Futuristic Sports Experimental) was a bold and sleek

■ LEFT *Honda's first-ever concept car was the FS-X, a sporting saloon (sedan) with advanced engineering and a sharply styled aluminium body.*

Electric and novel

For the 1993 Tokyo Show, Honda unveiled two further concepts. The first nailed its commitment to electric vehicles to the wall: the compact EVX predated the arrival of Honda's series production EV model, one of the first-ever ground-up electric cars. The second was the FSR, billed as "the ideal sedan for the 21st century". It was a technology car with such futurist goodies as active headlamps, radar braking, a message board for drivers following, reflective paint and a front-mounted camera for better visibility in adverse conditions. The wheel-arch

design clearly targeted at the Lexus and Infiniti luxury Japanese brands, which had had such success in America. Typically advanced in engineering terms, the FS-X sported a 3.5-litre VTEC V-six engine developing 280bhp, an all-aluminium body, four-wheel drive, liquid crystal sun visors and four airbags.

The little EP-X (Efficient Personal Experimental) was a curious, narrow tandem two-seater, also made entirely from aluminium. Powered by a 1.0-litre three-cylinder engine, it was claimed to be highly aerodynamic, efficient and safe if impractical.

■ ABOVE *Light weight, safety and aerodynamics were high on the agenda of the EP-X commuter vehicle.*

■ RIGHT *The EP-X was very compact, most notably in terms of width: the two passengers sat in tandem.*

treatment front and rear was novel, but the well-laid-out interior was more down-to-earth.

SSM stood for Sports Study Model, and this interesting 1995 show car was widely expected to enter production in modified form. It used NSX-style aluminium construction and ensured sharp handling through its front-engine/rear-drive layout: Honda claimed a perfect 50/50 weight distribution front-to-rear. One novel feature on the car was a central "spur", which separated the driver's and passenger's compartments and was claimed to improve rigidity significantly.

The SSM's power was supplied by a 2.0-litre five-cylinder VTEC engine, driving through a new electronic sequential-shift automatic gearbox derived from that in the NSX. The instrument pack was an LCD display with a card-style ignition system and push-button starter.

Another novelty in 1995 was the Side-by-Side, a racing single-seater with a 650cc V-twin motorcycle engine mounted alongside the driver. Weighing just 380kg (840lb), it was fast, superbly balanced and a possible production prospect.

■ ABOVE *Angular shapes realized in aluminium pointed the way ahead for Honda design. The passenger and driver were separated by a metal bar.*

■ ABOVE *SSM stood for Sports Study Model. Although it first appeared in 1995, its appearance at shows for a further two years fuelled speculation about possible production.*

■ RIGHT *Coupés have always been a strong suit at Honda, and this aggressively styled four-seater shadows the American-market Acura CL.*

I A D

■ BELOW *The spectacular Venus was a dramatically wedge-shaped piece of sculpture, yet was fully functional, based around a Lotus Elite engine.*

International Automotive Design was founded in Britain in the 1970s, but its real glory days did not arrive until the 1980s. Eventually, it opened offices in California, Detroit, Tokyo, Paris, Frankfurt and Turin and became one of those quiet operations behind numerous mainstream products.

From Alien to Venus

After a few innocuous design studies, IAD burst on to the world scene with "an attempt to 'out-Countach' the Countach", as the designer of the Alien described his work at the 1986 Turin show. As an exercise in attracting international attention to the young British design company, the Alien was incredibly successful – crowds surrounded the car all through the show. Eventually, IAD attracted many big names, including Fiat, Mazda and Volvo, who beat a path to its door for design work.

The Alien was a stunning, waspish supercar with a F16 fighter-style glass

canopy over the passengers. Its handlebar steering and centre console reinforced the jet-plane impression.

Further concepts followed thick and fast. The Impact and Interstate were outrageous developments of the off-

roader/leisure vehicle (sports-utility) genre. Then came the Venus, audaciously launched at the hallowed Tokyo Motor Show in 1989, and later made fully functional for a Turin debut the following year. The canary-yellow Venus (designed by Michael Ani) used a Lotus Elite drive-train in another wedge-shaped body, dominated by a table-like plateau to the rear and ingenious wheel covers. These almost completely shrouded the wheels, and had a bold yellow accent across one-quarter of the circumference. IAD was flooded with Japanese work following the Tokyo debut.

Another highly impressive exercise was the Royale, an imposing luxury express (grand tourer) with mature lines. The interior was perhaps its most striking feature, decked out with leather and high-tech equipment, including one of the most sophisticated hi-fi systems ever seen on a car.

■ LEFT *The Venus, launched at the 1989 Tokyo Motor Show, made a big impact for British-based International Automotive Design.*

■ RIGHT *IAD's Hunter was a go-anywhere vehicle with a complete lack of any glass or weather gear.*

Its 1992 Lancia Integrale-based Magia prototype was extremely well received but a hoped-for production run with Lancia never materialized.

Calling it a Daewoo

In addition to production cars, IAD had considerable input into other manufacturers' show cars; for example, it created the 1989 SRD-1 for Subaru, a mix of five-door estate (station wagon) and low-slung sportscar styles, which ITAL design's Giorgio Giugiaro described as "right for the future". Also, it came close to entering production with one of the world's first viable electric hybrid cars, the LA301, but this effort was ultimately doomed.

IAD was eventually overcome by financial problems. Half the organization was acquired by British design and engineering company Mayflower, while the original Worthing design office came under Daewoo's control. IAD's talented design tradition therefore lives on in numerous Daewoo production and concept cars.

■ BELOW *With the Royale, IAD presented a mature-looking four-door executive-class saloon (sedan).*

■ ABOVE *The intriguing white interior of the Royale featured advanced electronics, including an extremely powerful hi-fi system.*

■ RIGHT *Rear-seat passengers in the Royale were swathed in white leather and the latest in-car technology.*

ISDERA

German stylist Eberhard Schulz made his name in the 1970s with b+b, the famous and well-respected tuning-and-styling operation that produced so many upgraded Porsches. The pinnacle of b+b's work was undoubtedly the 1978 CW311 prototype, whose inspiration (the Mercedes-Benz C111) was clear. Fitted with a mid-mounted AMG-tuned 6.3-litre V-eight engine, many industry experts reckoned it had enormous promise.

■ BELOW *The Spyder's cockpit was topped off by twin head fairings. Power came from a mid-mounted Mercedes-Benz engine from 2.3 to 3.0 litres capacity.*

■ ABOVE *Isdera's first project was the Spyder 033, which caused a stir with its decidedly Germanic styling and speedster-type roof arrangement.*

Teutonic Spyder

In fact this promise was so enticing that Schulz set up a separate company to market a range of similar products. That was in 1983, and the first car to be produced was the Isdera Spyder 033.

The 033 mid-engined sportscar was as close to a dream car for the road as you could get. Its styling themes were very Teutonic: silver paint, strong forms coalescing into a muscular whole and an almost industrial theme throughout. Evocative head fairings nuzzled up behind the two passengers, who were

■ ABOVE *In cabin architecture, Isdera was very German. Colour schemes like this were all the rage in the 1980s, though hardly the highest expression of good taste.*

■ LEFT *Isdera's second model – and its most popular – was the Imperator. It looked very much like a development of Mercedes/Benz's CW311 concept car.*

■ LEFT *The Imperator was a very fast machine. In standard production form, it had a Mercedes-Benz 560SEC V-eight engine.*

the 1993 Frankfurt Show, the 112i Commendatore. Its development period was quite lengthy but resulted in a car that followed Isdera traditions, in other words the sort of supercar that Mercedes-Benz might have been making, if it hadn't had to deal with environmental issues.

The Commendatore was a fearsome beast. The predictable Mercedes V-twelve engine sat in the centre of a much more curvaceous body, but was tuned up to 400bhp. This meant a claimed top speed of no less than 212mph (341kph) and the sort of reliability you would never expect from other super-powerful sportscars.

protected from the elements only by a small wind deflector (there was no weather gear). They got in by hinging the doors upwards; the doors also took the wind shields up with them.

The 033 was powered by a Mercedes-Benz 2.3-litre engine. From 1989, this was replaced by a 16-valve 2.5-litre unit (195bhp) or a 3.0-litre six-cylinder.

Ferocious Dreams

Isdera's second model was the enclosed Imperator 108i, which was clearly derived directly from the b+b CW311 prototype, even down to its periscope for a rear-view mirror. The 108i had full gullwing doors and larger overall dimensions, and was altogether in a different league in terms of performance thanks to the fitment of the 5.6-litre V-eight engine from the Mercedes-Benz 560SEC. If you wanted even more

power, you could opt for the ferocious AMG 32V 6.0-litre engine: its 390bhp would take you to 188mph (302kph).

Isderas were built in tiny numbers: by 1990, less than 20 Spyders and no more than two dozen Imperators had been made. Not greatly increasing these numbers was a new model presented at

■ LEFT *The wedge-shaped profile of the Imperator was born in the 1970s but remained in production into the 1990s.*

■ BELOW *With an optional AMG 6.0-litre engine, the Imperator could reach a top speed of 188mph (302kph).*

ISUZU

The name Isuzu is known in the West
mainly through its successful off-road
vehicles and, even in Japan, Isuzu is the
smallest and least prestigious of the
domestic brands. It is all the more
amazing, then, that the company should
have such a brilliantly rich stream of
design talent at its beck and call, and
that it has produced, over the years, a
startling string of concept cars.

4200R – star of Tokyo

Although hints of Isuzu's dream-car
specialization were already evident in
the COA series during the 1980s, no
Isuzu dream car better illustrates its
talent than the 4200R, which was the
star of the 1989 Tokyo Show. Through its
General Motors connections, Isuzu had
close contact with Lotus in Britain, and
it was Lotus that, via Isuzu's Brussels-
based design office, essentially created
the 4200R.

Julian Thomson was the designer of
one of the cleanest shapes of this period:
well proportioned, elegant, unfussy and
free of gimmicks. Ex-Lotus man Simon
Cox was more adventurous with the
textured gunmetal interior, a two-plus-
two cabin entered by four cleverly
designed doors, the rear pair hinging
clear of the body and sliding backwards.

The intention was that under the skin
would lie a Lotus-developed version of

Isuzu's 4.2-litre V-eight quad-cam
engine, producing 350bhp. Other
technical highlights were four-wheel
drive, Lotus active ride, a head-up
display and navigation system. Sadly,
the 4200R never made production,
despite some encouraging noises.

Also at the 1989 Tokyo Show were two
home-grown concept cars, the Costa and
Multi-Cross, both based around the MU
(Frontera) 4x4 platform. The Multi-
Cross was a simple, rugged enclosed
car with interchangeable doors and
bumpers, while the Costa had a
nautical theme.

Como – the F1 pick-up

Nothing could have been as nautical as
the 1991 Nagisa show car, for this was
actually a boat! In fact it was an
amphibian, capable of cruising in the
sea as easily as transporting its two
passengers through the Tokyo rush hour
– a completely daft notion.

■ **LEFT** *Simon Cox created the startling Como,
a car that combined supercar and pick-up
styles over a Lotus V-twelve Formula 1
mechanical package.*

■ ABOVE *The XU-1 was a great 1993 exercise combining the rugged form of Isuzu's specialist off-roaders with sportscar-type scissor doors.*

■ ABOVE *The Multi-Cross was a 1989 attempt at an off-roader with interchangeable panels, based on the Isuzu/Vauxhall Frontera.*

No such derision awaited the Como, even though the idea of a Formula 1-powered pick-up may have seemed odd. Styled by Simon Cox, it used a mid-mounted Lotus V-twelve F1 engine and had a very short nose, gullwing doors and a pick-up rear deck. At the same 1991 Tokyo show but from Isuzu's California studio came the Terraza, an urban car powered by a ceramic engine and featuring a fifth wheel at the back for parking manoeuvres.

Group B rally cars, rally-raiders and the Citroën 2CV were all cited as influences by the designer of Isuzu's 1993 VehiCross, Simon Cox. Although its styling looked almost like science fiction, it was extremely well designed and thought out. Its chunky shape impressed executives so much that a feasibility study was carried out, and the VehiCross became a production vehicle with amazingly little modification within three years (bypassing the similar-looking but larger 1995 Deseo show car). There was no such happy fate in store for a dreamy fellow off-roader created by Californian stylists, the Trooper-based XU-1.

■ ABOVE *Is it a boat or a car? The Nagisa combined the two in one sublimely silly package.*

■ BELOW *Widely admired, the VehiCross was such a satisfying concept that Isuzu had the courage to re-engineer it for series production.*

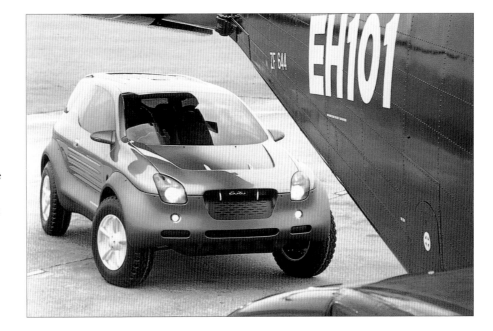

ITAL DESIGN

■ BELOW *Giorgetto Giugiaro's very first project after forming Ital Design was the Manta, a mid-engined coupé based on Bizzarrini parts.*

Giorgetto Giugiaro's background in a family of artists helped him in his career as an "artist" of automotive forms. Even though his design career has encompassed such diverse areas as menswear, watches and pasta, his first passion has always been cars.

Giugiaro, the young art master

Aged just 17, Giugiaro joined Fiat's styling wing under Dante Giacosa and, two years later, accepted a job at Bertone and went on to become its youngest-ever head of styling.

In 1965, he left Bertone to head up Ghia and within three years had grown confident enough to set up his own consultancy with another ex-Fiat design and engineering expert, Aldo Mantovani. The office started in Turin but moved six years later to Moncalieri. Ital Design offered not only styling but also all the

■ LEFT *Geometric forms dominated the Boomerang and set Ital Design's agenda for two decades.*

■ RIGHT *Giugiaro cites the Tapiro as one of his most successful ever designs from a technical point of view.*

services needed to bring a design to production, and soon manufacturers were flocking to his door.

As Ital Design, Giugiaro styled dozens of shapes for mass production, including the VW Golf, Maserati Bora, Lotus Esprit and BMW M1, all notable for an exceptional cleanliness of line. Ital Design has also produced some of the most admirable dream cars during its years, and has been highly influential in setting future trends.

Ital Design's very first project was the 1968 Manta, a dramatic coupé for the Italian specialist car-maker Bizzarrini. This was followed by sportscar designs

for Alfa Romeo (the 1969 Iguana and the 1971 Caimano), Abarth and Volkswagen (the VW-Porsche Tapiro and the Karmann Cheetah).

Boomerang and other prophecies

In 1972, the same year that Giugiaro designed the Esprit for Lotus, he also produced what many regard as his most extraordinary sportscar design, the Maserati Boomerang. This car, based on the Maserati Bora, pushed the frontiers of the accepted limits of car design. At only 42in (107cm) high, it was so low that the passengers were forced to become acrobats to get in, and the

■ LEFT *The Lancia Megagamma of 1978 was a pioneer of the MPV form which grew up in the 1980s.*

■ ABOVE *Wind tunnel testing became one of the most important factors in the car design process. Here the Medusa is put through its paces.*

15-degree angle of the windscreen was the steepest rake you could achieve and still be able to see out. The wedge shape originated from a point in the nose, expanded to the base of the windscreen and extended to a geometric tail. Only the lower glass in the door opened.

As Ital Design extended its base of clients in the late 1970s, its concept cars became more prosaic, but the 1976 New York Taxi and the 1978 Lancia Megagamma were prophetic, proposing the idea of a compact, high-roof car with an adaptable interior layout – an MPV ahead of its time. In 1980, Giugiaro's Medusa showed a way forward in aerodynamics, proving it was possible to create a very clean four-door shape. This Lancia Montecarlo-based proposal boasted a Cd figure of just 0.263, then the most aerodynamic road car ever.

In 1984 Ital Design created the Etna for Lotus, which was at one stage earmarked for production. This was a supercar fitted with a stillborn Lotus four-litre V-eight 360bhp engine in the centre of the car. The contrast between its upper and lower halves was

emphasized by using thin, black-painted pillars, creating the impression of a transparent dome. The similar-looking Ford Maya from the same period was intended as a genuine production possibility and was full of practical features. It also had a removable targa top.

■ ABOVE *With a front end almost indistinguishable from the Etna, the Ford-based Maya struggled to find its own identity.*

■ ABOVE *The Medusa proved that a long-wheelbase four-door design could be extraordinarily aerodynamic.*

■ RIGHT *The Etna was built for Lotus in 1984, and should have become that company's first-ever V-eight supercar, but it was not to be.*

ITAL DESIGN

■ ABOVE *The main design feature of the Asgard was its extensive use of glass.*

■ LEFT *Outlandishly different, the Machimoto combined the joys of the motorcycle and car worlds. All passengers sat astride seats arranged in rows.*

Giugiaro struck out on a startlingly original course with the 1986 Machimoto, a hybrid of motorcycle and car elements. Although it looked like a cabriolet and used VW Golf GTI mechanicals, passengers sat astride twin rows of seats, rather like a motorbike, but the layout allowed seating for up to nine people. It could be steered either by a conventional wheel, by handlebars or by vertical hand grips. Another novelty was the prominent design of the wheel spats (skirts).

A similar feel recurred in 1996 with

■ ABOVE *The Aztec was a typically adventurous idea for a four-wheel-drive two-seater sportscar.*

■ LEFT *No less than three similar concepts were all based on Audi components: from front to back, the Aztec, Aspid and Asgard.*

the Formula series. This was a concept for multi-adaptable bodies to be fixed over the same structure. Giugiaro initially showed two ideas: the Formula 4 with its demountable speedster body and aero screens, and the Hammer with its open sides, split windscreen and more conventional seating. Neither was especially handsome but they both provided yet more evidence of his original thinking.

Aztec, Aspid and Asgard

More creativity arrived in a trio of designs produced in 1988. Each of the Aztec/Aspid/Asgard triplets shared a

■ ABOVE *More effort was expended on the Nazca than any other Ital Design concept car, but then this was a highly sophisticated BMW-engined supercar.*

common design theme and similar Audi mechanicals but had very different intentions. The most notable design element was the so-called "service centres" on either flank, which included sculptured gauges, read-outs for fluid levels and intricate compartments for tools and flashlights.

The Aztec was a four-wheel-drive two-seater with symmetrical but separate compartments accessed by doors, which hinged along a central point. The passenger's dashboard looked like the driver's, but the "steering wheel" was in fact a handle and the "instrument panel" was a screen to display car information on request.

The Aspid was identical to the Aztec up to the waistline and was a coupé version, which featured complex double-

■ ABOVE *The Nazca theme was later developed by Ital Design to become the Spider, with an open roof.*

■ BELOW *The Nazca M20 boasted conventional doors with gullwing window flaps. Some observers would have liked to see the Nazca enter production as a BMW.*

camber (dual-angle) glass, fold-up roof sections and conventionally hinged doors. The Asgard was a one-box eight-seater design, which broadened the extent of the extraordinary glass surfaces seen on its smaller coupé sister.

With the 1990 Kensington, Ital Design suggested a future shape for a Jaguar saloon, and used Jaguar's V-twelve engine. The Jaguar chassis was left untouched but a modern yet recognizably "Jaguar" body was created. Interestingly, the windscreen was sited so far forward that it needed to be removed to dismantle the engine.

Nazca, Columbus and Firepoint
The Nazca of 1991 was probably the most talked-about of all Giugiaro's concept cars, and there was speculation that it might enter production as a BMW. Everyone remembered the

ITAL DESIGN

Giugiaro-styled BMW M1 supercar and the Nazca seemed to be the natural successor. It had a mid-mounted BMW V-twelve engine and styling, which inspired dozens of magazines to run cover stories. Entry was by conventional doors and flip-up side windows. Despite the fact that the Nazca went through two further evolutions, including a Spider version, BMW was adamant that it would not build such a supercar.

BMW did donate another V-twelve engine for the stupendous Columbus of 1992, which celebrated the 500th anniversary of the discovery of America. This was a huge machine: 19ft 6in (6

■ RIGHT *A BMW V-twelve engine sat underneath the immense Columbus, designed to whisk large parties of VIPs around at high speed.*

metres) long, 7ft (2.2 metres) wide and over 6ft 6in (2 metres) high. Its specification was equally grand: four-wheel drive, four-wheel steer, mid-mounted 300bhp engine and 20in (50.8cm) wheels. The interior was split into two compartments: the driver sat on a higher level with up to eight additional seats"below" in three rows.

In 1994, Fiat asked all the major Italian design houses to create a special body for the Punto (which was a Giuguaro design in the first place). Ital Design's interpretation was the Firepoint, a novel two-plus-two coupé with aircraft-inspired aerodynamics, such as the teardrop roof and reversed windscreen pillars. The side and rear windows could be removed, cleverly creating a roadster.

■ ABOVE *The electric-powered Biga was a minute little box capable of seating five people.*

■ BELOW *A V-ten engine sat amidships in the two-plus-two Cala prototype.*

■ ABOVE *Ital Design teamed up with Lamborghini to create the Cala, which was interestingly styled and could have become a production model.*

Cala and Legram

Lamborghini asked Ital Design to create a new two-plus-two targa sportscar that would slot in as an entry model below the Diablo, and so it created the Cala, which came tantalizingly close to production. The compact mid-engined two-seater used a brand new Lamborghini V-ten engine capable of phenomenal performance. Stylistically, its detail cues came from the Miura, though the overall shape was more of a wedge. Its advanced construction consisted of an aluminium chassis clothed in carbonfibre body panels.

The 1996 Legram was an almost unrecognizable development of the Formula "infinity project" begun by the Formula 4. On the basic Formula platform went an elegant sporting four-seater body with an exceptional Cd figure of just 0.25. A transparent dome of glass stretched from the windscreen base to the rear window, broken only by aluminium cross-beams. Another outstanding feature was the treatment of the rear lights, which looked like horizontal slits.

Ital Design's back catalogue of dream cars is bewilderingly complete and belies the relative youth of the company. Equally impressive is the depth of its engineering expertise and the extent of its penetration into the design of production models. In all cases, Ital Design has been a trailblazer of ideas and an initiator of clean design principles and high-quality execution.

■ RIGHT *Firepoint was the name given to Ital Design's Fiat-sponsored proposal on the Punto.*

■ ABOVE *The idea behind the Formula project was to have bodywork that was easily interchangeable. This is the Formula 4 sportscar.*

■ ABOVE *The Legram proved that the Formula concept could produce a more serious outcome. Note the intriguing use of glass surfaces.*

■ RIGHT *By changing a few of the upper panels, you could create the Formula Hammer. Some thought that this design idea was seriously compromised.*

MAZDA

Of all the Japanese manufacturers, Mazda has historically been the most adventurous in its production programme. Witness such extremes as the Wankel-engined Cosmo, the lithe RX-7 and MX-5 sportscars and the amazing AZ1 micro-gullwing coupé.

Alongside Nissan and Toyota, Mazda was one of the first of the Japanese show car originators, with cars like the 1970 RX 500. An early impact was achieved in 1981 when its MX-81 show car made its debut. The interest was the stylist, Bertone.

Mazda charted its direction with dream cars like the MX-03 of 1985. With the interesting MX-04 (1987) Mazda showed its ingenuity: this was a four-wheel-drive chassis shown with interchangeable bodywork – Mazda suggested roadster, coupé and buggy styles.

One of the three versions of the micro AZ550 Sports prototypes shown at the 1989 Tokyo show led to a production vehicle, the AZ1, a sports projectile designed within Japan's micro-car laws (maximum length 126in (320cm), maximum engine capacity 550cc).

Type A had a strikingly simple shape dominated by its glassy gullwing doors. Type C did not actually conform to the

■ ABOVE LEFT *Mazda teamed up with Bertone to create its 1981 show car, the MX-81. Typically clean lines combined with a large glass surface area.*

■ LEFT *There was no steering wheel as such in the MX-81, merely an oblong "track" surrounding a TV display.*

■ ABOVE *Interchangeable bodywork provided the 1987 MX-04 with a choice of buggy or sports styles, the latter prefiguring the MX-5 production roadster.*

■ ABOVE *Mazda's cute and tiny AZ550 Sports Type A actually became a production model (the slightly modified AZ1).*

■ LEFT *The AZ Type B was a funny little creation designed with removable roof panels for open-topped motoring.*

■ RIGHT *Despite being only just over 10ft long, the Type C AZ550 looked like a proper Group C racing-car.*

legal micro size requirements, but it was an amazing concoction looking like a toy-sized Group C racer, complete with a slanted front profile, large radiator intake and rear spoiler. Type B was perhaps the runt of the litter with its awkward humped lines.

Japanese Jekyll and Hyde

The 1989 Mazda TD-R was the first car to combine two potentially burgeoning fields, melding the apparently incongruous worlds of sportscars and off-roaders. Its nod to the sportscar world was its mid-engined two-seater layout, turbocharged 1.8-litre engine and ventilated disc brakes. Its off-roading alter ego emerged in permanent (full-time) four-wheel drive, minimal front and rear overhangs and deep sills. Joining Jekyll and Hyde was a novel wishbone suspension system, which could adjust the TD-R's ground clearance between 5in and 9in (130mm to 230mm).

Mazda's 1991 HR-X did not win any awards for styling, but that was not its main *raison d'être*. The HR-X pioneered a hydrogen-powered variant of Mazda's twin-rotor Wankel engine, which could

■ LEFT *Mazda's M2 division created a variety of special bodies, such as this M2 1008 coupé conversion for the MX-5. The headlamps are fixed behind cowls.*

also power an on-board hybrid electric motor. The bulky hydrogen tank was sited under the floor, but whatever its advantages, hydrogen looked an unlikely future power source, especially in such an outlandish shape as the HR-X's.

Centre stage at the 1995 Tokyo show went to the RX-01 prototype, a vision of a future, lighter, cheaper RX-7 sportscar. The rotary engine was retained, without the sequential turbocharging of the

contemporary RX-7, but with dry-sump lubrication and improved breathing – still good for 220bhp. It weighed only 2425lb (1100kg) and had aluminium suspension based on the MX-5.

Mazda was also unique in having an operation called M2, a dedicated design company based at its own office block in Tokyo. It created all sorts of alternative bodywork and engine modifications on existing Mazda cars, notably the MX-5.

■ ABOVE *Rotary power remained a Mazda forte, and the 1995 RX-01 provided a lightweight sportscar vision of its possible future.*

■ RIGHT *The TD-R successfully combined elements of sportscar and buggy themes: mid engine, four-wheel drive and variable ground clearance.*

MERCEDES

The C111 was not one project but five. This supercar blueprint was first shown in 1969, and was outside Mercedes-Benz's normal frame of reference.

A laboratory on wheels

Mercedes-Benz described the C111 as a "laboratory on wheels", and some were actually used on the road. Some of the features included gullwing doors, leather-trimmed cockpits and even air-conditioning.

■ BELOW LEFT *Breaking diesel speed records at Nardo in 1978: the aerodynamic C111/112 achieved an average top speed of 200mph (322kph).*

■ BELOW RIGHT *Mercedes-Benz show cars often anticipated forthcoming production cars. The F-200, despite its scissor-type doors and joystick controls, prefigured the new S-Class.*

The first example had a glassfibre body over a steel chassis and was fitted with a mid-mounted triple-rotor Wankel engine with fuel injection. That expanded to four rotors in the second generation C111 of 1970 – said to be good for 370bhp and 180mph (290kph). In its third form, a 3.0-litre five-cylinder turbodiesel engine was fitted, and the C111 immediately took all existing world speed records in the diesel class.

Further evolutions, with quite different bodywork, took more records: over 200mph (322kph) with a diesel engine (and 12 hours at an average 195.3mph (316kph)) and still more records with a 500bhp 4.8-litre twin-turbo V-eight.

There was a follow-up to the C111, logically called the C112. It appeared at the 1991 Frankfurt Show as a mock-up, by which time Mercedes-Benz was convinced that the market for such a supercar was not right – probably correctly, given Jaguar's experiences with the XJ220. The C112 would have been a stunning 6.0-litre V-twelve-powered mid-engined supercar. Mercedes even took orders for it (700 were received), but it returned them all.

Mercedes thinks small

As Mercedes-Benz began to diversify, it launched various concept vehicles to

■ OPPOSITE *Perhaps the most famous of all Mercedes-Benz concept cars was the C111, which first appeared in 1969 with a triple-rotor Wankel engine.*

■ ABOVE *Presented at the 1997 Frankfurt show, the F-300 Life-Jet was an amazing three-wheeler designed to lean into corners to simulate the behaviour of motorbikes.*

■ ABOVE *The AAV excited many show-goers because here, said Mercedes-Benz, was a clear indication of how the M-class (M320) off-roader would be.*

■ RIGHT *The stylish and highly textured interior of the AAV was typical of the boldness of concept cars.*

■ OPPOSITE *What might have been: the C112 was going to be a production V12 supercar but instead it was shown simply as a dream car in 1991.*

■ ABOVE *As the climate for supercars became more favourable in the mid-1990s, Mercedes-Benz and AMG built this stunning CLK GTR as a homologation road/race special.*

prepare the public for future changes. One example was the 1991 F100 MPV show car, paving the way for Mercedes' forthcoming V-class MPV.

The next obvious prediction of future models was the Vision, shown in 1993. For Mercedes-Benz this was a very radical concept, its first-ever small car. For the rest of the world it was also radical, featuring a ground-breaking layout of an engine sited so that it would move underneath passengers' feet in a head-on collision – good for driver and front-seat passenger safety, said Mercedes. By 1997 it was ready to launch the A-class, whose profile differed little from the Vision.

The same thing happened with the SLK (shown in concept form in 1994 and later somewhat diluted, particularly in the design of the headlamps and twin head fairings), the F200 (previewing the 1998 model S-class coupé) and especially the AAV, Mercedes' prototype 4x4, which fired so many imaginations – the eventual M-class road car was very staid in comparison. Perhaps most radical of all the designs was the F-300 Life-Jet trike, which leant into corners via computer control. Young, fresh and innovative, this exciting concept car brought to Mercedes a new sense of fun and experimentation.

MITSUBISHI

Mitsubishi burst into the dream-car arena with its HSR series which originated in 1987. Active ride, four-wheel drive and four-wheel steering may not have been very original in the concept car world but the fact that 295bhp and 186mph (299kph) were available from a 2.0-litre turbo engine certainly was.

A show-stopping car

Show-goers were impressed by the HSR's dramatically skirted shape, sophisticated electronics and novel seating, which swung out with the doors.

■ ABOVE *Mitsubishi's reputation for high-technology solutions reached new heights with the 1995 HSR-V, whose aerodynamics were claimed to have been inspired by dolphins.*

The stunning 1989 HSR II follow-up was officially only ever meant as a rolling test bed for technology and ideas, but the amazing shape attracted virtually all the attention, an aim that Mitsubishi surely intended, since it featured widely in corporate advertising campaigns. Mitsubishi called this project a Control Configured Vehicle, in other words a machine stuffed with computers and electronic displays. At various points around the body were flaps and wings whose position was controlled by computer so that airflow was optimized in any given situation.

■ ABOVE
Biodynamic suspension and an elastic (flexible) tail spoiler were two very '90s features of the HSR-IV.

■ RIGHT *The HSR-III was strikingly styled and also technically advanced, with electronic suspension, four-wheel drive and four-wheel steer.*

■ ABOVE *This tiny bespectacled Lynx off-roader had an engine of just 660cc capacity.*

■ ABOVE *Some people likened the oddball mS 1000 saloon (sedan) to a modern-day duo-tone Morris Minor. Certainly it reflected a trend towards "retro" design.*

■ RIGHT *At the 1995 Tokyo Show, the Gaus offered a modern solution to adaptable luxury multi-purpose transport. The gullwing doors were more fanciful.*

Less noticed but perhaps more significant at the 1989 Tokyo Show was the RVR leisure car. Its novel retractable windscreen and targa roof were striking, and the latter made it into production in the Japanese-market RVR (Space Runner), which arrived in 1991.

The HSR evolved into a third generation in 1991. More compact but equally striking in its powerfully styled presence, the HSR III boasted electronically controlled suspension and traction control and a new 177bhp twin-cam 1.6-litre V-six engine. More far-fetched was the fitment of twin levers on the steering wheel in place of controls for the automatic transmission.

Inspired by dolphins

More outlandish 1991 Tokyo debutants were the mS 1000 and mR 1000 pairing. Catching the tidal wave of Japanese interest in all things "retro", the mS 1000 was an utterly bizarre two-tone curve-haven with a tiny chrome grille. It had two doors on the left and only one on the right, while the stubby little boot (trunk) led Mitsubishi to call it a "2.5 box" car. The mR 1000 looked more feasible: a two-seater targa-roofed runabout (commuter car), spoiled by flying buttresses at the rear and ugly tail lamps.

The proportions shrank even further in 1993 with the presentation of the tiny 101in- (257cm-) long, two-seater Mum, powered by a 500cc 30bhp engine, and the Lynx, an off-roader designed around Japan's micro-car regulations – meaning maximums of 660cc and a 130in (330cm) overall length.

By 1993 the HSR series was in generation IV, its styling ever more avant-garde, notably its elastic (flexible) aerotail rear spoiler. More significant was its "biodynamic" suspension, which became a production reality in the Galant.

Even more bells and whistles sprouted from the HSR-V in 1995, from elastic stabilizers to a vibrating under-floor, which was "a revolutionary way of reducing drag inspired by the skin of dolphins".

■ LEFT *Even by Japanese standards of miniaturization, the Mum was truly Lilliputian. It had a 500cc engine.*

NISSAN

Like most Japanese car-makers, it took Nissan almost two decades to refine its dream-car programme into something that was relevant and palatable for a worldwide audience. Early efforts, such as the 1970 126X, were characterized by dubious extremes and a certain lack of sophistication. However, Nissan did have some interesting ideas, including inflatable passenger airbags as early as 1971.

The dream car that catapulted Nissan into a more serious arena was the MID-4, which was a major Nissan project. It was first seen in 1985 as a Ferrariesque pure show car, but had matured by 1987 to look like a credible exotic rival for Porsche.

It was engineered around a 330bhp longitudinal 3.0-litre V-six twin-turbo engine and boasted four-wheel drive and four-wheel steering. There were serious noises about this becoming a production prospect as a new Nissan supercar, probably with a V-twelve engine and two-wheel drive, ready to do battle with Ferrari et al. That plan was scotched as the times did not favour such "hypercar" projects, although the production 300ZX of 1989 was hailed as "the first Japanese supercar".

The elegant 1986 CUE-X and ARC-X of 1987 also marked a new maturity.

■ LEFT *With a 330bhp twin-turbocharged V-six engine mounted amidships, the MID-4 promised much, although its styling was perhaps a little bland.*

■ ABOVE *The cleanliness of line and sensibility of proportion won many admirers when Nissan displayed its CUE-X in 1986.*

■ LEFT *The ARC-X of 1987 was a sophisticated precursor to Nissan's luxury-car programme Infiniti.*

Here was a pair of super-sleek, beautifully proportioned four-door saloons, which were also highly aerodynamic. The ARC-X featured four-wheel drive, four-wheel steer and a staggering array of electronics.

Pike dreams

Perhaps Nissan's most celebrated dream cars were the so-called Pike series of boutique models. Nissan set up a sub-division to manufacture special models,

■ OPPOSITE *The MID-4 was one of the more significant Japanese dream cars of the 1980s, as at one stage it was slated to become a production rival for Porsche and Ferrari.*

■ ABOVE *The first of the so-called Pike series was the curious Be-1, a retro-styled small car, which was so well received that it went into limited production.*

■ ABOVE *If the Be-1 evoked the 1960s, the Pao plunged further back to a utilitarian post-war era of flat glass, exposed hinges and sober lines. Again it was sold in small series.*

or "niche" cars in marketing language. The first of these was the Be-1, shown at Tokyo in 1985 and so well received that it went into production 18 months later. Its Mini-style round headlamps and retro-styling cues overcame the fact that it was based on the dowdy one-litre Micra, and it was widely admired.

Then in 1987 came the Pao (a 1940s-style runabout) and the humorously named S-Cargo, a bizarre arch-shaped van, which achieved tremendous popularity. Another design from this series (but destined not to go into production) was the 1989 Chapeau, a curious glass-house car, which looked somewhat like a telephone kiosk (booth) on wheels.

Perhaps the most charming of all the Pike cars was the Figaro, initially shown as a concept car but actually put into production. This heralded a new era of "retro" design in the car world, for here was a 1940s-style chrome-and-round-headlamps little car. Some details were appealing, like the electric canvas roof and chromed CD player; others were more dubious, like the all-white interior and toggle switches, which looked like Victorian cutlery. Also, it may have had the appearance of a sportscar but its 1.2-litre Micra engine and automatic transmission did nothing to make it behave like one.

■ LEFT *The humorously named S-Cargo was a brilliantly styled high-roof van.*

■ RIGHT *With the Figaro, Nissan exploited nostalgic yearnings for a different age. Production was very limited, and the 20,000 run was vastly over-subscribed.*

NISSAN

■ ABOVE *This bold, retro, ultra-simplistic fascia comes from a 1989 concept called the Chapeau. While the interior was admirable, the exterior looked preposterously like a telephone kiosk (booth).*

■ ABOVE *The Rasheen brought a unique boxy style to the sports utility market. When it was shown as a concept car, western tastes were not motivated, but in production the Rasheen became a hot seller in Japan.*

From Boga to Duad

Nissan lost the plot a little with the 1989 Boga, its idea of a new city car. The concept was clever, to fit a four-door shell with luxury car space into an overall length of a supermini (compact), but the 1.5-litre Boga's style missed the

mark, and it perhaps got less attention than it deserved. Similar styling marred the 1991 Cocoon six-seater, whose party piece was a wake-me-up system: when it sensed that the driver was drowsy, it would spray a refreshing scent into the cockpit.

Nissan's 1989 UV-X was more down-to-earth, a neat one-box shape designed by Yoshio Maezawa, stylist of the 300ZX sportscar. Apart from being tipped to look like a future Bluebird (it didn't), its main feature was computer-controlled adjustable pedals and steering.

The 1991 TRI-X show coupé looked disappointingly back to the 1980s, and was clearly targeted at an American audience; this sort of thing reappeared in 1993 with the Marcello Gandini-styled AP-X. Much more engaging was its quirky Duad show car, which revived in spirit its 1987 Saurus. Intended as a modern interpretation of the immortal Lotus 7, it weighed merely 1035lb (470kg). Its quirkiness stemmed from the fact that the 1.0-litre engine was

■ LEFT *Although it looked perhaps like a dumpy VW Beetle, the FEV II had a more serious purpose, exploring city car possibilities.*

mounted alongside the driver, forcing the passenger's seat to be sited 15in (38cm) further back. Nissan hoped to launch the Duad as another in its Pike boutique series, but this never happened.

From Rasheen to Trailrunner

A different fate awaited the Rasheen, shown at Tokyo in 1993. This extremely box-like concept, described as "a totally new type of four-wheel-drive wagon",

actually made it into production. Its compact dimensions, practical Sunny mechanicals and characterful style endeared it to Japanese drivers, and led to a crew-cab-type (four-door pick-up) show car called the XIX in 1995.

Combining two-seater drop-top excitement with four-seater practicality was how Nissan described its 1995 AA-X, but the awkwardly colliding shapes looked uncomfortable, even if the idea itself was sound: to combine sportscar and family-car modes.

Nissan followed a happier path with its 1997 4x4 concept vehicle, the Trailrunner. Sporty styling crossed the bridge between the coupé and off-road worlds, and a unique design feature was a prominently displayed sliding spare wheel in the tail. Its 190bhp 2.0-litre engine and sequential six-speed CVT gearbox also promised a sporty temperament.

■ ABOVE *Nissan's designers were called upon to complete the R390 GT1 project in a short space of time.*

■ BELOW *To homologate the R390 for Le Mans in 1997, a tiny batch of road-going cars was built for discerning customers.*

OGLE

David Ogle founded his own industrial design company in 1954 and decided to branch out into car design (and indeed manufacture) in 1960 with a four-seater GT coupé based on Riley 1.5 mechanicals, but only eight were made. More successful was the pretty SX1000 coupé of 1962–64, an extremely curvaceous glassfibre body based on Mini parts.

Ogle also designed the very handsome SX250 body on the chassis of the Daimler SP250. This was shown at the 1962 London Motor Show and impressed British specialist company Reliant so much that it was modified to become the

Reliant Scimitar coupé. Ogle then took the Scimitar and made a Triplex GTS estate (station wagon) special with a rear-end made of Triplex heat-absorbing glass. This car became the property of HRH Prince Philip for a time.

Tragically, in 1962 David Ogle died at the wheel of an SX1000, effectively ending the company's manufacturing life. Direction was taken over by Tom Karen, an innovative Czech-born designer. He was responsible for some effective designs, most significantly the Reliant Scimitar GTE sports estate.

The tangerine bug

The car of which Karen was most proud was the 1970 Bond Bug, a highly individual-looking three-wheeler based on a Reliant chassis. In many respects it was ground-breaking with its hinging canopy, its fixed, moulded-in seating, its use of aircraft-style black decals. Intended as a cheap fun car, it was available in only one colour – bright tangerine! Despite this, several thousand were sold.

Perhaps Ogle's most ambitious project was an Aston Martin DBS-based

sportscar created for the 1972 Montreal show. This sharply styled coupé featured much Triplex Sundym (tinted) glass, a green corduroy-and-leather interior with seating for three (the rear passenger sited diagonally behind) and brushed-steel highlight panels. Most remarkable of all was the rear-lamp panel, which had 22 circular lights. Many of these were sequential indicators, which flashed outwards in the direction you were turning; six others were for braking, the severity being indicated by the number of lamps lit.

Ogle went on to design a number of further one-offs such as the Princess 10-20 Glassback, the Mogul (which was a full-size version of a child's toy car Ogle had already designed), a modified Vauxhall Astra and various taxi projects.

Ogle Design's automotive work gradually dwindled away into occasional ventures such as the Project 2000 and a proposal for an updated three-wheeler to celebrate 21 years of the Bond Bug. Today, Ogle's car connections are at best tenuous as it concentrates on other industrial design work.

■ ABOVE *The Bond Bug was the most characterful of all Ogle Design's cars. A front-engined three-wheeler, it was available in only one colour – bright tangerine.*

■ BELOW *Ogle's Aston Martin DBS Special was state-of-the-art in 1972, featuring large Sundym (tinted) glass areas and brushed steel. Two examples were built.*

■ ABOVE *To get into the Bug, the roof canopy had to be lifted up, taking the sidescreens (windows) with it.*

■ RIGHT *The tail of the Ogle Aston housed no fewer than 22 lamps for braking, reversing and rear lighting.*

PEUGEOT

■ LEFT *Peugeot's best-known dream car is the Oxia, and not without reason. Its low, wide face was distinctively Peugeot.*

With Paul Bracq at the helm, Peugeot has had an illustrious design influence. Its true dream-car programme began with the Quasar at Paris in 1984. Based on the 205 Turbo 16 rally car, it was a formidable compact mid-engined sportscar with four-wheel drive and 200bhp. Its styling was light and forward-thrusting, its interior dramatically encased by a red roll cage.

The spectacular Oxia

Without a shadow of doubt, Peugeot's most important ever show car was the Oxia, first seen in 1988. Unlike many other dream cars, the Oxia was a fully-functioning prototype, quite capable of stunning levels of performance, as Peugeot proved during numerous well-documented test runs.

In its looks, too, the Oxia was absolutely spectacular. It was designed in-house by Gerard Welter and incorporated such Peugeot elements as low-cut headlamps, horizontal grille and rampant lion badge. The flamboyantly rakish and wide shape was realized in lightweight carbonfibre, and was topped off by an adjustable rear spoiler to help stability.

On a high-tech menu to set technophiles' palates slavering were a four-wheel steering system with variable weighting (variable assist), permanent (full-time) four-wheel drive (via a Ferguson viscous coupling), six-speed gearbox, anti-lock brakes, electronically controlled axle differentials and automatic

■ LEFT *With a turbocharged race-spec engine developing 680bhp, Peugeot was justified in claiming a top speed in excess of 200mph (322kph).*

■ BELOW *Based on the rallying Peugeot 205 T16, the mid-engined Quasar not only looked purposeful, it had the power and punch to carry out that purpose.*

■ ABOVE *The 1984 Quasar demonstrated that Peugeot's in-house design team had plenty to offer.*

■ ABOVE *Opening the Proxima's roof canopy revealed an uncompromisingly scarlet cockpit.*

tyre-pressure monitors. Inside, traditional leather blended with solar-powered air-conditioning, a personal computer, a sound system described as "intergalactic" and a navigation system.

The basic engine was Peugeot's familiar 2.85-litre V-six but monstrously modified to full race specification with twin turbochargers to develop no less than 680bhp. Peugeot claimed – with justification – that the Oxia was capable of a top speed of 205mph (330kph).

Ion, Asphalte and Touareg

At the 1994 Paris Salon, Peugeot presented the Ion, an urban study vehicle powered by electricity. Only 11ft (3.3 metres) long, its monobox style was compact and modern, yet could fit four adults. Perhaps the main novelty was the total absence of door handles; to get in, you pressed a sensitive area on the rear wing – with your hip if your arms were full – and so released the locks. The same system worked for the large rear hatch.

"Crazy" was how some professionals described the extraordinary 1996 Paris Salon debutante called the Asphalte. The front-end picked up Peugeot design themes – wide snout, narrow headlamps – but toward the back-end things got very strange. The rear track was extremely narrow, so that from the side it looked like a three-wheeler with a pinched-in tail. The ultra-smooth topless profile promised sizzling performance, but strangely Peugeot opted to install a mere 1.6-litre engine and an automatic gearbox.

The Touareg off-road buggy stood out because of its mighty, even frightening wheels, straight off a science-fiction film set. One interesting quirk was its choice of power: four electric motors, one for each of those Tonka-toy wheels.

■ ABOVE *All attention focuses on the moon buggy wheels and tyres with Peugeot's 1996 Touareg concept car.*

■ LEFT *Although it looks like a three-wheeler, the Asphalte in fact had a pair of rear wheels, which were very narrowly set.*

PININFARINA

At only 5ft (1.5 metres) tall, Battista Farina's nickname of Pinin – "kid" – is altogether fitting; so much so in fact that the name stuck and late in life he changed it officially. He founded a design centre of true genius, which his son Sergio continues to run from Turin, the capital of Italian and indeed world car design. He is among the great names of car design.

The pinnacle of car design

To cast back over the company's long list of production greats confirms the consistency of quality and proportion that distinguishes his work. From the

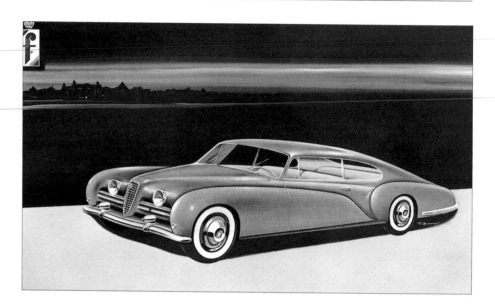

revolutionary 1945 Cisitalia (displayed in the New York Museum of Modern Art) to present-day Ferraris (which, since 1952, have almost exclusively carried the Pininfarina badge), the mark of genius is evident in the little blue 'f' badge with a crown on top. In between are dozens of designs for Alfa Romeo, Fiat, Peugeot, Honda, Rolls-Royce and many others.

■ ABOVE *Farina's fascination with aerodynamics was evident in the extraordinary PFX prototype of 1960. Its diamond-wheel footprint helped reduce frontal area and thus drag.*

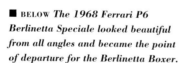

■ BELOW *The 1968 Ferrari P6 Berlinetta Speciale looked beautiful from all angles and became the point of departure for the Berlinetta Boxer.*

■ ABOVE *Despite a fascination with flowing shapes, aggression had its place in Farina's school of thought, as the Can-Am-inspired 1968 Alfa Romeo P/33 shows.*

■ LEFT *Pure sculpture on wheels is the almost inevitable description for the extraordinary Modulo of 1970, based on a Ferrari 512S.*

■ ABOVE *The 1969 special-bodied Alfa Romeo 33 was one of the great shapes of the 1960s, inspiring a generation of supercars.*

Pininfarina's dream cars are united by one theme: a flowing shape and perfect proportions. While others explored geometric shapes, Farina was inspired by the way snow in the Italian mountains was shaped by the winds, and the wind-cheating shapes of all his cars owe something to this stimulus. Others claimed that Farina said his ground-breaking stimulus came from well-formed female shapes.

The art of aerodynamics
Pininfarina was one of the first companies to install a wind tunnel (in 1972). A direct result of testing in this environment was the PF-CNR family-size car, which achieved a world record Cd figure of 0.161 and had a curious banana-shaped form: Pininfarina proved it could be practical by creating a version with air intakes, lights and mirrors (though the Cd figure increased to 0.23).

Not that aerodynamics was a new art-form, as the 1960 PFX proved. This extraordinary befinned, egg-shaped car even used a diamond-shaped-wheel footprint in its search for wind-cheating efficiency. A seminal aerodynamic study was the 1967 Dino 206SP, based on a racing Ferrari. It featured adjustable front and rear spoilers and gullwing doors. In the 1960s, Pininfarina experimented with some wild shapes, yet none of them had the glitzy fripperies of American show cars. Farina's designs were always classically elegant. One of the most influential was undoubtedly the 206 Dino and later Ferrari 365 P Special Berlinetta, which led directly to the Dino production car.

■ ABOVE *The Modulo had enclosed wheels and a canopy, which slid and cantilevered forward, drawing attention to what was in fact a brilliantly simple shape.*

■ RIGHT *One of Pininfarina's most admired production designs was the Fiat 130 Coupé. Here is the Maremma, an estate (station wagon) development study.*

PININFARINA

Farina Ferraris and Alfas

Pininfarina was always Ferrari's favoured couturier, not surprisingly in the light of such brilliant dream-car designs as the 250/P5 Berlinetta and the superbly clean P6 Berlinetta. Possibly the zenith of this golden era of mid-

■ LEFT *A world record co-efficient of drag was recorded for this windtunnel-honed CNR – just 0.161.*

■ ABOVE *No doubt disappointed that Jaguar had failed to replace, in spirit, the great E-Type, Pininfarina produced this 1978 Jaguar proposal, based on the XJS.*

engined fantasy were the Ferrari 512 prototype and very similar-looking Alfa Romeo 33 prototype, whose exquisite sculpted sides, gullwing doors and ultra-low profile clearly inspired the Boxer and Countach of the following years to come.

Exploring the wedge school of design was the 1968 Alfa Romeo P/33 Roadster, based on the mid-engined racing 33. This was intended for impact, as evidenced by the row of six headlamps, front stabilizing fins, cut-down wind deflector (airdam) and prominent rear spoiler.

With the 1970 Modulo, based on the ultra-rare Ferrari 512S racer, the very extremes of sportscar design were explored to the absolute limit. Its very low bodywork formed an almost flat, almost symmetrical arc and was made by joining separate upper and

lower halves together. The prominent waistline strip – so low that it could almost be called an ankle-line – was allowed to run uninterrupted right around the car, including the wheels. These were covered with spats (skirts) which incorporated cut-outs in their tops. To allow entry, a one-piece canopy cantilevered forward.

Honda, Peugeot and Jaguar

Equally dramatic was the 1984 Studio HPX, a mid-engined supercar using a 2.0-litre Honda Formula 2 V-eight engine. Its striking shape was highly aerodynamic, partly owing to ground effect technology and the curious extended canopy (a Cd figure of 0.25 was claimed).

■ LEFT *Ferrari was always the keenest on Pininfarina's shapes, and the Turin design house pushed the boat even further with this supremely elegant Pinin prototype of 1980.*

■ ABOVE *Honda is another firm with a long association with Pininfarina. This Honda HPX had an extended glass canopy for optimized airflow.*

■ RIGHT *The 1985 Peugeot Griffe 4 was a good example of Pininfarina's restrained good taste, even in its show cars.*

Widely admired for its simplicity was the 1976 Peugette, an exercise in virtual symmetry of form. In fact the front and rear bodywork sections were completely interchangeable, and hinged up in identical fashion. The lights were housed in the bumpers, and the interior was marvellously unadorned. Its mechanical basis was the Peugeot 104.

The 1978 XJ Spider showed what the fabled Jaguar E-Type might have become. On the basis of a Jaguar V-twelve engine, a timelessly elegant body was created, picking up the E-Type themes of an oval front air intake and a profile, which bulged over the front and rear wheels. Jaguar's boss Sir John Egan fell in love with the XJ Spider and even developed its themes with the intention of launching an F-Type Jaguar. This was scotched, but it's enlightening to see how the current XK8 picks up many of the XJ Spider's details.

Perhaps even more elegant than the Jaguar study was Farina's Ferrari-based study for a four-door car of two years later, called simply Pinin. In proportion it was supremely correct, and its sharp yet soft-edged style predicted the way many cars would be designed in the late 1980s. Ferrari never officially made a four-door car, and after seeing the Pinin many observers felt they ought to have done so.

Mythos, Chronos and Ethos

After doing several relatively "sensible" concept cars (such as the 1988 HIT based on Lancia Delta HF mechanicals), it was time in 1989 to try something more ambitious, and the Mythos was the result. The designers at Pininfarina based the car on the Ferrari Testarossa.

■ ABOVE *The HPX was typically clean but atypically geometric in its wedge-shaped profile.*

■ BELOW *Disguising the extreme girth of the Ferrari Testarossa was a challenge that the 1989 Mythos addressed.*

PININFARINA

■ ABOVE *To fit six people in the Ethos III, two rows of three seats had to be installed.*

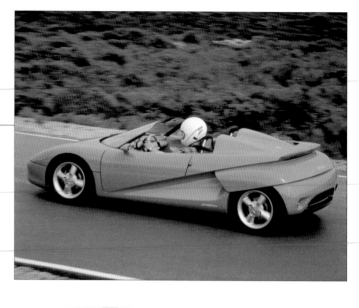

■ RIGHT *Showing an originality of thought, the remarkable thing about the Ethos roadster was that at one stage Honda seemed likely to put it into production.*

The 1991 Chronos was a serious stab at a two-seater coupé based on Lotus Carlton/Omega running gear. Pininfarina wanted to persuade General Motors to go into production with the Chronos but ultimately did not succeed, probably because the shape was slightly disappointing for a Farina.

The same cannot be said of the 1992 Ethos, which also seemed capable of becoming a highly significant production car. It used an Australian-made Orbital 1.2-litre two-stroke engine mounted amidships and a sequential five-speed gearbox.

The Ethos body was penned by Stephane Schwarz, and was a steeply raked pure sportscar with deeply indented sides, virtually cycle-type rear wings, head fairings and a bold, stark interior with twin silver bars for a dashboard. At one stage, Honda looked likely to produce the Ethos, but the Oribital two-stroke engine unfortunately suffered many delays and the project faltered, despite the appearance of an Ethos II coupé.

The Ethos III of 1994 attempted to reinvent the city car. Into a body barely longer than a Fiat Cinquecento, Pininfarina managed to squeeze six seats – two rows of three with the middle seat offset. Crucial to the compact dimensions was the tiny 1.2-litre

■ ABOVE *The Ethos III was another extremely clever design. The body was smaller than virtually any car on the market, yet it could seat six people.*

■ BELOW *Argento Vivo is Italian for "quicksilver", and this Honda-based study was certainly mercurial in character. It combined "retro" and hi-tech themes.*

■ LEFT *Highly polished aluminium panels gave the Argento Vivo its silvery name. Note the hardtop.*

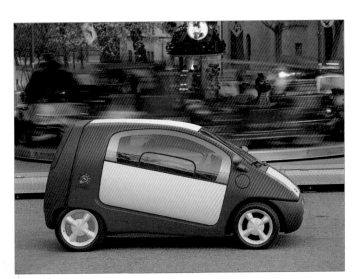

■ RIGHT *As a fully functioning project using Honda Vigor and NSX components, the Argento Vivo might have made a practical production proposition, but Honda had irons in other fires.*

three-cylinder Orbital two-stroke engine. Lightweight aluminium kept the weight at 1720lb (780kg) and helped create 63mpg (100kpg) fuel economy.

Honda and Fiat

A 16-year co-operation with Honda was finally cemented in 1995 with the Argento Vivo sportscar concept. This was a power-top roadster with striking polished aluminium boot and bonnet (trunk and hood), blue bodywork and wide use of plywood. It was notable for a folding transparent roof, which could also be left in a targa position. Unfortunately, Honda was already developing a similar car in the SSM, and the Argento Vivo remained a scintillating prototype.

For the 1996 Turin show, Fiat asked various stylists to come up with ideas on its Bravo/Brava. Pininfarina's concept was the Song, a compact MPV with a multi-adaptable interior and more than a hint of off-road influence in its roof rails, clipped overhangs and chunky wheels. At the same show was the Eta Beta, powered by a hybrid petrol/electric (gasoline/electric) system and featuring a tail section extendable by 8in (20cm) for extra carrying capacity.

In 1997 Pininfarina continued its rich tradition as the world's leading design house; its advanced Nautilus saloon (sedan) car concept for Peugeot proved that it was still very much on the leading edge of car design.

■ LEFT *The cleverest feature of the hybrid/electric Eta Beta was rear bodywork that could fold out to increase luggage capacity.*

■ BELOW *Tarina's concept car for 1997 was the Nautilus, an extremely handsome four-door saloon (sedan) based on Peugeot components.*

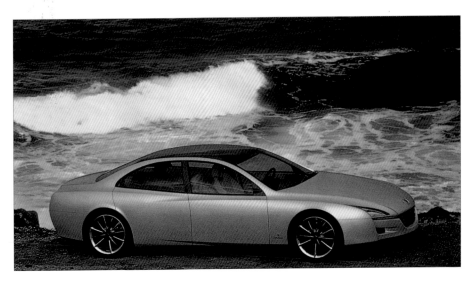

RENAULT

The largest French car-maker founded its fortunes on comfortable, conventional and often rather boring family cars. It certainly did not go in for outlandish styling concepts and dream cars, preferring merely to hint at a little chic in its road-car offerings, which were deliberately designed for the masses.

That old attitude changed dramatically with the arrival of Patrick Le Quément as head of design in 1987. "We sell to people, not the masses" he said, and Renault's approach to its

■ ABOVE *Renault was one of the great show-car exponents. Here is an impressive selection of concept cars, starting with the 1990 Laguna (front right) and ending with the 1995 Initiale (second car in, top right)*

■ LEFT *The Zoom's headlight shows Renault's attention to stylized details.*

production car design was transformed with such innovative cars as the Twingo and Mégane Scenic.

Le Quément cleverly instituted a policy of producing show cars – and names – which clearly predicted future production Renaults, a trick he picked up during 17 years with Ford. In this way a lot of publicity was gained for Renault's show cars and the public was prepared for the revolutionary shapes and ideas of the next generation.

Le Quément banished the ghosts of such uninspiring experimental Renaults as the Vesta 1 and 2 (both super-economy cars) and the Eve Plus, an

■ ABOVE *Created by Renault-owned Matra, the tiny Zoom was a vision of a future electric city car.*

■ RIGHT *The Zoom's party piece was an ability to fold its rear under, shortening its overall length by 21.5in (55cm).*

■ LEFT *The moon-buggy Racoon was a go-anywhere vehicle in the widest sense: it could also take to the water!*

■ ABOVE *The Scenic concept car of 1991 (left) led directly to the production Mégane Scenic car (right).*

aerodynamic efficiency saloon (sedan). The first project he oversaw was the 1988 Mégane, an elegant three-box saloon with such essential 80s equipment as four-wheel steering, intelligent suspension and a turbocharged engine. It was highly aerodynamic, notching up the very impressive Cd figure of 0.21.

From Twingo to Zoom

A tremendous exponent of the one-box design embodied by Renault's Espace, Le Quément's team created the much-vaunted Twingo, having earlier shown a larger one-box design called the Scenic at the 1991 Frankfurt show. This evolved into the production Mégane Scenic of 1996, a car that can genuinely

be said to have revolutionized one segment of car design.

In 1990, Renault first used the name Laguna on an ultra-sporty open two-seater dream car. Underneath the swoopy shape lay a mid-mounted two-litre engine (210bhp), and the cockpit could be covered by a solid tonneau. The concept of a completely open mid-engined sportscar obviously struck a chord at Renault because, some five years later, the very similar Sport Spider actually entered production.

Renault's subsidiary, Matra, developed the 1992 Zoom prototype, a startling electric two-seater. Quite apart from its arresting egg-like appearance and scissor-type opening doors, the

Zoom could amaze onlookers by pulling its rear wheels in and under its body, shortening the overall length from 104.3in to 82.7in (265cm to 210cm) – handy for parking in that tight Paris spot.

From Racoon to Initiale

Renault described its adventurous 1993 Racoon concept car as "an amphibious go-anywhere vehicle". It had four-wheel drive, hydraulic jacks to elevate ground clearance, a watertight body and completely amphibious capability. Its mechanical specification was not retiring either: a twin-turbo 262bhp V-six engine and six-speed gearbox.

Equally striking was the Twingo-based Argos roadster of 1994. This show

■ RIGHT *Launched at the 1994 Geneva Motor Show, the Argos was a startlingly original design from design chief Patrick Le Quément. The "piano lid" is actually the hinging boot.*

■ FAR RIGHT *Argos details: retractable screen, doors and mirrors, exposed rivets and a single rear seat with hi-fi gear.*

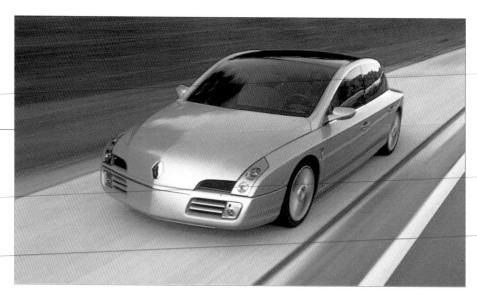

RENAULT

car really gave rein to Le Quément's vision of breaking with the "organic" shapes of the early 1990s. The Argos was full of industrial, Bauhaus-style detailing and little technological tricks such as ignition-activated swivelling door mirrors, drop-down doors, a folding 1920s aeroplane-style windshield and a piano-like opening rear lid. Interior textures in shades of green, cork and silver made a visual feast.

If anyone thought one-box design was

■ ABOVE *The 1995 Initiale was a projected future Renault limousine of superb elegance and, thanks to a detuned Formula 1 engine, deeply impressive performance.*

■ ABOVE *Avant-garde detailing from the rear end of the Initiale.*

■ LEFT *Hard edges and soft curves balanced the Initiale's presence superbly.*

■ BELOW *The Modus and Ludo were Renault's 1994 vision of electric-powered city transport of the future.*

the only way to go, then Renault banished that idea with the Ludo concept car at the Paris Salon in 1994. The two-box Ludo had a very adaptable interior with foldable, removable seats and a huge interior volume; it anticipated similar treatment for the 1997 Renault Clio.

With the elegant Initiale (1995), Renault signalled a way ahead for luxury cars, and stole some of the thunder of Ford's edge-design programme. The Initiale was a super-saloon (high-performance sedan) powered by a detuned Formula 1 engine (claimed top speed was 190mph, or 306kph), yet had accommodation for four people. The tapered nose and tail recalled the style of the 40CV, Renault's prestige model in the 1920s.

Fiftie and Pangea

To celebrate 50 years of the highly successful Renault 4CV, Renault's design team produced the Fiftie for the

■ ABOVE *Novel interior treatment in the Fiftie included wickerwork (woven) trim and curious stacks at either end of the dashboard.*

■ RIGHT *Retro and resolutely modern influences met in the Fiftie concept car of 1996.*

Geneva show in 1996. This was a concept car out of the normal stream. Certain elements of the 4CV were recognizable – the curved roof-line, the raised bonnet (hood), the air intakes for a rear- mounted engine – but this was definitely not a retro design.

The fact was that the Fiftie had a Sport Spider chassis and was an ultra-modern two-seater. It marked the first fitment of Renault's new 1149cc engine (which would later power a revised Twingo), and was sporting in slant. The roof could be wound back and then folded down to make a virtual convertible, while the interior was a delightful blend of natural textures and curious "stacks" at either end of the dash. Particularly striking was the treatment of the lights, both front and rear, the tail-lamps "evoking waving flags," said Renault.

At the 1997 Geneva show, Renault displayed a concept van called the Pangea, which clearly predicted the shape of its forthcoming Kangoo utility/family car. In spirit, this was greeted as a revival of the long lost, greatly mourned Renault R4, as its boxy shape recalled the car that was France's best-selling machine of all time. Again this was no throwback, however, but was resolutely looking forward – like all of Renault's concept machines.

■ LEFT *The Fiftie's roof slid back and then down on to the rear deck. Note the rear lights – evocative of flags waving in the wind, said Renault.*

■ BELOW *The Pangea concept vehicle (complete with trailer) was exhibited as a high-tech remote office facility.*

RINSPEED

Based in Zurich, Switzerland, Rinspeed's main stock-in-trade has always been outrageously fast and furious conversions based on regular production performance cars. It started out turbocharging Volkswagen Golfs, then moved on to Porsches, with which it really made its name. One of its most celebrated conversions was a "droop-snoot" front-end on a 911, a style that Porsche itself later adopted for its own car designs.

Usually Rinspeed altered the aesthetics of its base cars, typically upgrading wheels and tyres, adding a body kit, installing pop-up or high-intensity headlamps, injecting leather and wood into the interior and stacking up a monster hi-fi system.

Eventually, it also turned to other, even more exotic projects. The Veleno was a mutated, 550bhp nitrous-oxide-injected Dodge Viper, for example, while Rinspeed also modified a Bugatti EB110 visually and mechanically.

Then, at successive Geneva Motor Shows, it surprised and occasionally shocked the world with its avant-garde dream cars. Unusually, these design extremes were actually offered for sale in series (regular production) at stupendously high prices, admittedly, at last offering some home-grown competition for the king of automotive couture extraordinaire, Lausanne-based Franco Sbarro.

This achievement was realized by teaming up with American operations TLC and Panoz, which actually

■ LEFT *Called the Veleno, this heavily modified Dodge Viper looked different and – thanks to a nitrous oxide-charged 550bhp – felt quite different too.*

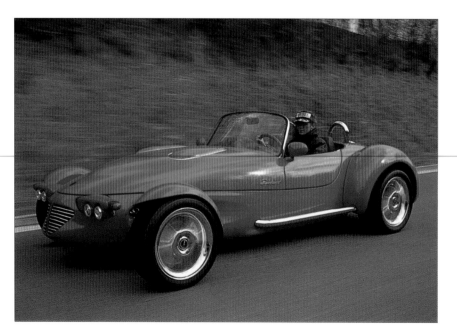

■ LEFT *The Roadster was a sportscar in the old-fashioned sense of the word. Note the strange "eyes-on-stalks" headlamp treatment.*

■ ABOVE *Fitted with a Ford Mustang V-eight engine, with up to 305bhp on offer, the Roadster was a very rapid machine.*

■ BELOW *The timelessly graceful lines of the 1930s were underscored by ultra-low-profile tyres and a supercharged 320bhp V-eight engine.*

■ ABOVE *The Yello Talbo was inspired by the classic 1930s Talbot-Lago but brought kicking and screaming into the '90s – hence the association with electro band Yello.*

manufactured the cars; Rinspeed was responsible for the outlandish additions to the coachwork.

Stars of the Geneva show

The first of the Geneva series was the 1995 Roadster, a sort of updated Lotus 7/AC Cobra cross-over with tiny doors, a narrow windscreen, separate wings and evocative roll-over hoops. It was the nose that grabbed all the attention: extraordinary "eyebrows" sprouted from either side of the jut-forward snout, housing compact, underslung double headlamps and indicator units sited on their tips. The impression was of the

face of some wild banshee, an effect augmented by the colour of the show car – bright orange!

Powering the Roadster was a five-litre Ford Mustang engine, available in two states of tune. The R version had 218bhp while the ferocious SC-R got 305bhp. Rinspeed claimed performance figures of 160mph (258kph) and 0–60mph (96kph) in 4.4 seconds for the faster SC-R version.

The following year (1996), Rinspeed presented the Yello Talbo, whose name derived from TLC's existing Talbo model in the USA and the urban/electro-pop music group Yello, which endorsed the

car. Inspired by a 1938 Talbot-Lago 150SS design by Figoni & Falaschi, the Yello Talbo resolutely brought the shape into the 1990s. Its supercharged V-eight engine developed 320bhp.

In 1997 came the strangest Rinspeed yet, the Mono Ego. Many questions were raised at its Geneva show debut. If this was a Yankee-style hot rod, why did it have a Hyundai engine (an "experimental V-eight") and Hyundai Coupé lights? Why one seat? Why was a famous French fashion designer involved? No satisfactory explanation was received, but that was in a way the point: a total defiance of logic.

■ RIGHT *An implausibly long bonnet (hood) covered an equally implausible engine – a V-eight from Korean company Hyundai.*

■ ABOVE *No one was quite sure what to make of the Mono Ego, a bizarre mix of haute couture fashion and American hot rod.*

SBARRO

Franco Sbarro is an Italian who emigrated to Switzerland in the 1950s and went on to become that country's most famous car-maker and one of the design world's most adventurous figures. His extraordinary work ranges through tiny electric cars, exquisite replicas of great classics, racing-cars, imaginative one-offs and innovative supercars.

He shot to fame in 1969 when he transformed a Lola T70 racing-car into the world's fastest road car, but his name

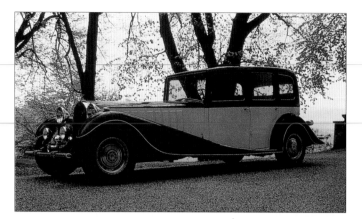

■ LEFT *Franco Sbarro's extraordinary dynasty kicked off with exquisite replicas such as this Bugatti Royale, which used two Rover V-eight engines joined together to make a V-sixteen.*

■ ABOVE *The Super Twelve may have looked like a hatchback with a simple paint job, but underneath it all lay two Kawasaki motorcycle engines making a 12-cylinder unit.*

■ ABOVE *Looking like a slice of Swiss Gruyère cheese, the Challenge was a very rapid sports coupé offered with Porsche or Mercedes engines.*

■ BELOW *The Challenge may not have been particularly handsome, but it was dramatic in every way.*

became widely known through a string of replicas, including BMW 328, Bugatti Royale and Ferrari P4.

His "Super" series was particularly headline-grabbing. Its least spectacular members were the Super Eight, which looked like a VW Golf but had a Ferrari 308 chassis and engine, and a Porsche 928-engined Golf. The first of the series, the 1982 Super Twelve, was simply outrageous: an unassuming hatchback with two Kawasaki six-cylinder motorcycle engines joined together amidships for a single engine developing 240bhp.

Another project in a similar vein was the Robur, a very compact, 130in (330cm) long car with a 200bhp mid-mounted Audi turbo engine and a fifth wheel, which proved useful for pulling the rear-end into tight parking spots.

The Challenge came close to being a mass-production car by Sbarro's standards, since seven have been built to date. This uncompromising wedge-shaped car, first seen in 1985, looked like a slice of Gruyère cheese and was

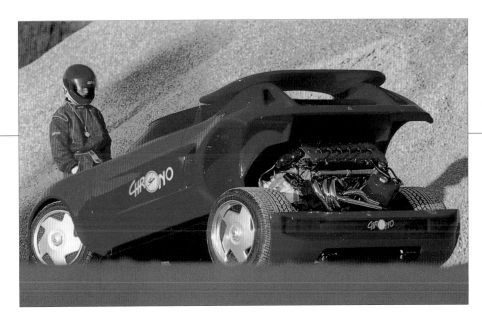

■ RIGHT *Sbarro's unconventional approach to improving engine access is plain for all to see in the Chrono.*

claimed to have a Cd figure of just 0.25. The doors folded forward for entry. Initially the Challenge was offered with a twin-turbo Mercedes V-eight engine, but later cars had Porsche engines mounted in the rear. All were capable of storming speeds – up to 180mph (290kph) was claimed.

"Throw out the hubs!"

Proving that extremes did not have to relate to speed alone, Sbarro's 1987 Monster G was a phenomenal all-wheel-drive concoction. It was not the four-wheel drive but the wheels themselves that impressed: they were taken from a Boeing jet! These made the Monster sit

some 7ft 5in (2.3 metres) tall, and the 350bhp Mercedes-Benz 6.9-litre V-eight was needed to get those wheels moving.

"Throw out the hubs!" exhorted Franco Sbarro at the 1989 Geneva show when he released on to the world a major innovation: the hubless wheel.

The concept of a wheel without a centre to it had a sound theoretical basis, as Gordon Murray confirmed. The idea was that the wheel rotated around bearings actually in the rim. Having the drive and braking applied directly to the rim meant greater rigidity, less weight, less

■ ABOVE *The Astro was relatively toned down by Sbarro's standards. It had a Ferrari engine and curious little projector headlamps under the windscreen.*

■ ABOVE *With its ex-Boeing aeroplane wheels, the Monster G was ideal for assaulting urban wastelands or indeed other forms of desert.*

■ LEFT *The hubless wheel was invented by Franco Sbarro. It actually worked, as this motorcycle proved.*

torque reaction, less axial and radial strain and perfectly vented braking. Sbarro had experimented with such wheels on a motorcycle a few years before; however, it was obvious that much more development was required, and this innovative scheme was left on the shelf.

Nevertheless, the Osmos show car, which incorporated the hubless wheel, was popular at motorshows. Cleanly styled, somewhat soberly perhaps for Sbarro, it boasted a 12-cylinder engine.

SBARRO

■ LEFT *Under the long bonnet of the concept Isatis lay a BMW 5.0-litre V-twelve engine.*

■ ABOVE *In characteristic red overalls, Franco Sbarro sits in one of his creations, the Urbi electric city car.*

Chrono, Isatis and Oxalys

The 1990 Chrono hinted at its purpose with Swiss watch badges dotted around the body. This was a car designed to go from 0–60mph (0-96kph) in the shortest possible time. Weighing just 1430lb (650kg), the same as a 2CV, yet powered by a 500bhp BMW M1 engine, it could do "the sprint" in 3.5 seconds. In a typical Sbarro touch, the whole car hinged in the middle for access to the engine.

For the 1991 Geneva show, Sbarro presented an interesting twin-chassis supercar. The V-twelve engine and gearbox, beam chassis and suspension were attached to the body by six hydraulic links. In theory, these allowed the body to be insulated from the chassis, which meant that a supremely comfortable ride was possible without sacrificing the firmness of the

suspension. The body could also be jacked up at will. Wild by anyone else's standards but shy by Sbarro's, the 1993 Isatis was based on the V12-powered BMW 750iL. The main interest lay inside, its steering wheel featuring a centre-mounted rev counter (tachometer) and speedo.

The next year came the Oxalys, an intriguing cocktail described as "designed by the young for the young". Underneath its smart exterior – designed by Espace Sbarro students – lay a 340bhp BMW M5 engine and Porsche 911 rear suspension and brakes. One novel feature of this

■ LEFT *Like virtually every Sbarro design, the 1995 Alcador was a fully functioning car capable of being driven in anger.*

■ ABOVE *With its muscular, sci-fi "shoulders" protecting the occupants, the Alcador had a 400bhp Ferrari V-twelve engine.*

"back-to-basics" roadster was a modern version of a dickey (rumble) seat – a convertible pair of rear seats.

Issima and Ionos

The main attraction of the 1996 Issima lay under its long, Alfa-badged bonnet. Nestling there were a pair of Alfa Romeo 3.0-litre six-cylinder engines joined to make an in-line twelve with 500bhp on tap. Its smart styling was admired by Alfa's own styling boss, Walter da Silva.

According to Franco Sbarro's students, who designed the 1997 Ionos, this was how a latterday Lancia Stratos should be. Following Sbarro's joining of two Alfa engines to make a straight eight, the Ionos had two Lancia Kappa five-cylinder units joined together to make an upturned V-ten layout, with a Porsche gearbox between the banks. Transmission was Porsche four-wheel drive. The "crash helmet" window profile was reminiscent of the original Stratos.

Also at the 1997 show was a pair of sportscars called the Formule Rhin and Be Twin. They were conceived to teach rich kids how to drive and were fitted with two sets of controls. The 1320lb (600kg) Formule Rhin had a ferocious 200bhp Peugeot 3.0-litre V-six engine behind the seats, while the Be Twin Lotus, under 990lb (450kg), had Elan-style backbone chassis, stressed mid-mounted engine (a 140bhp 1.6-litre unit from the Citroën Saxo Cup racer), self-ventilating disc brakes and double-wishbone front suspension.

■ ABOVE *Yet another piece of radical engine surgery saw two Alfa V-six engines being joined together to create an Alfa V-twelve in the Issima.*

■ LEFT *The Issima's interior was typically clean, unfussy and devoid of ornament.*

■ LEFT *The 1997 Ionos was Sbarro's view of a latter-day Lancia Stratos.*

■ BELOW *Sbarro founded a design and engineering school, and the Oxalys was just one of the projects realized by his students.*

TOYOTA

While most Japanese firms turned to European design houses for their innovative designs, Toyota struck its own course. The 1969 EX III was a case in point. Here was a sleek coupé, which advanced the dream-car ideal as much as the Europeans. Its sleek shape carried over to its ultra-smooth undertray (underbody), making it very aerodynamic.

■ ABOVE *Toyota's 1987 FXV-II prototype was typical of the characterless concepts produced by Japan in the 80s.*

■ ABOVE *It may not have been a great beauty to behold, but the 4500GT marked a brave tour de force for Toyota's design and engineering teams.*

Advanced technology, maturing design

Like most Japanese makers, Toyota's dream cars struggled to find an identity until the 1980s, when advanced technology and maturing design teams began to enhance the impact of its concept machines, such as the 1984 FX-1 with its electronic suspension, cantilevered doors and variable valve timing.

On Toyota's stand at the 1987 Tokyo show was a dream car that made it to production. The little gullwing AXV-II reappeared two years later as the Sera. It may only have been a Starlet underneath, but its character was made stimulating by its expansive glass bubble top – the glass in the doors curved round to form part of the roof.

One of the greatest technical *tours de force* of all time was the verdict on the 4500GT show car of 1989. Its Lexus-based V-eight engine had five valves per cylinder, the gearbox had six speeds, the suspension was variable and the run-flat tyres had pressure sensors on board.

■ ABOVE *Born out of the AXV-II prototype, the Sera was a rare example of a concept car making it into production.*

■ BELOW *The point of the AXV-IV was to reduce weight, and its advanced construction meant a total mass of just 990lb (450kg).*

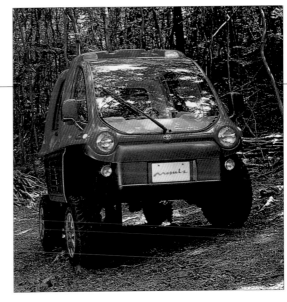

■ ABOVE *With a Cd figure of just 0.20, the AXV-V had an aerodynamic profile equivalent to that of an aeroplane.*

■ RIGHT *With suspension that was adjustable on each side (and even a half-track option instead of wheels), the Moguls turned mountains into molehills.*

Novelties included LCD shutters for the vertically stacked headlamps and sun visor, ultra-sound wing mirrors to clear water droplets and a Noise Canceller, which emitted signals of opposite phase and amplitude to eliminate noise "booms". Although the 4500GT may not have looked very pretty, all five that Toyota built were fully sorted road-going machines.

Concepts of all sizes

The AXV III concept car was merely a taster for the forthcoming Carina, while the 1991 AXV-IV was far more interesting, mainly for its construction, in ultra-lightweight aluminium,

magnesium and carbonfibre; even the springs were plastic. Immensely strong yet incredibly light (just 990lb or 450kg), the little coupé-style commuter car was fitted with a 64bhp two-cylinder 800cc two-stroke engine.

Mega Cruiser is not a subtle name, but then this was not a subtle car. Presented at the 1993 Tokyo show, it was a monstrous off-roader, 16.4 feet (5 metres) long, with a 4.1-litre truck engine. Following a good reception, it actually made it into production as one of the world's widest cars – all 7ft 1in (2.17 metres) of it.

The AXV-V of 1993 combined aerodynamics with advanced direct-

injection engine technology. Toyota claimed a Cd figure of just 0.20 – equivalent to an aeroplane – which helped to give it remarkable fuel consumption. Other technological innovations included air suspension, an anti-collision automatic brake system, touch-shift transmission and LCD monitors.

In response to a new wave of roadsters from MG, Fiat and BMW, Toyota unveiled its MRJ prototype at the 1995 Tokyo show. Actually designed by Toyota's Brussels design office, it was the company's first-ever open mid-engined car. The roof was a so-called "aerocabin" hardtop, which retracted electronically at the flick of a button.

■ ABOVE *Over 7 ft wide (2.1 metre), the four-wheel-drive, four-wheel-steer Mega Cruiser was actually sold on the Japanese market as the most expensive car around (costing 20 million yen).*

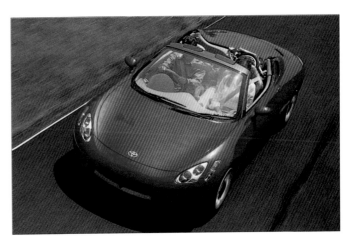

■ ABOVE *The very pretty MRJ was a mid-engined styling exercise and Toyota's first-ever open mid-engined car. It paved the way for a future generation of convertible MR sportscars.*

VW

One of the most vaunted of all 80s concept cars was Volkswagen's Futura, created by Professor Ulrich Sieffert. A one-box Golf-sized car – years before the Mégane Scenic made the genre popular – it was full of ideas.

The car that parked by itself

The gullwing doors were purely for show effect, of course: the notion of two-piece doors, of which the upper half were gullwing and the lower half dropped into the sills, was hopelessly impractical.

■ RIGHT *If the gullwing doors of the Futura were perhaps gimmicky, even more so was its ability to park itself via electronic monitors.*

■ BELOW *The idea behind the Vario was that any body could be fitted on to a common platform. This is the Vario I open four-seat buggy.*

Another novel city car proposal was the three-wheeled Scooter of 1986. Based on a Polo drivetrain, it was a lightweight, good-looking shuttle capable of 125mph (201kph). The two-seater interior included a dash-mounted briefcase!

At the 1991 Geneva show, VW presented another new concept called Vario. Two styles were displayed, to show how different the bodywork could

■ BELOW *The Vario II was an alternative bodywork proposal created by design students for VW.*

The mostly glass upper dome was equally striking.

More significantly, the direct-injection petrol (gasoline) engine was years ahead of its time. Aided by a G40 supercharger, the 1.7-litre engine was very economical and very clean.

The Futura's main party piece was its four-wheel steer system. Based on a Golf rear axle turned through 180 degrees, it provided plenty of fun when you wanted to park. Thanks to sensors fitted for restricted visibility and electronic throttle and transmission, the Futura could wriggle into a parking space all by itself, manoeuvring back and forth on its own.

■ LEFT *VW explored new territory with the Chico, a city car capable of being propelled by a variety of power sources.*

■ ABOVE *A commuter car with three wheels? The Polo-engined Scooter actually made a lot of sense, and was quick into the bargain.*

■ LEFT *Nothing less than the rebirth of the Beetle was how Volkswagen presented the Concept 1, styled by VW's California studio.*

be on the same platform. VW actually planned to sell a platform (based on a lengthened Golf Synchro 4x4) on which specialists could create their own bespoke (dedicated) bodies. However, VW's own efforts – admittedly designed by VW students – were uninspiring, and, not surprisingly, little more was heard of this novel idea.

The Beetle reborn

It was a design nucleus in VW's studio in California which created the car that stole all the thunder at the 1994 Detroit show – nothing less than the rebirth of

the legendary Beetle. Called Concept 1, it took the rounded themes of the 60-year-old Beetle and brought them into contemporary fashion, with bold Bauhaus curves and giant wheels.

The technology under it was modern, too, deriving from the Polo, and that meant front-wheel drive (or even four-wheel drive) and a front-mounted engine. The reaction to the Concept 1 (and its convertible brother, which

appeared at Geneva three months later) was so overwhelmingly positive that VW took the bold decision to engineer a production version for 1998. The shape and dimensions were changed and the basis (mechanicals) switched to the Golf MkIV, but in spirit and broad brush strokes the new Beetle was essentially a concept car born in the flesh.

Following up that media event was always going to be difficult, and efforts like the Noah gullwing MPV study, while striking, have not had such an impact.

■ RIGHT *A handome Cabriolet (convert-ible) version of the Concept 1 was displayed at Geneva in 1994 and looked equally likely to enter production.*

ZAGATO

Zagato belongs to a select band of Italian coachbuilder dynasties. It is one of the oldest of all, founded by Ugo Zagato in 1919 in Milan, and has an illustrious past. Its heyday undoubtedly came in the 1950s and 60s when it created superb coachbuilt bodies for Ferrari, Alfa Romeo, Fiat, Maserati, Aston Martin, Bristol and Lancia.

Brothers Elio and Gianni Zagato set up a new factory in 1962 and eventually expanded into other areas such as electric and armoured cars. A unique Zagato characteristic is the "double-bubble" roof, originally intended to clear the heads of passengers in its very low bodies, but this has since become an

■ LEFT *The Alfa Romeo-based Zeta 6 was a high point for Zagato: well proportioned, smooth and purposeful in appearance.*

■ ABOVE *The Zeta's cowled instruments were in deference to the traditional Alfa Romeo style.*

■ LEFT *The undoubted beauty of the Zeta 6 impressed Aston Martin enough to commission Zagato for one of its own projects.*

From Zeta 6 to Raptor

The 1983 Zeta 6 can be singled out as perhaps Zagato's best recent design. This two-plus-two coupé was based on the 2.5-litre Alfa Romeo GTV-six. Chief stylist Giuseppe Mittino extracted a classically graceful style from this project and gave it the Zagato trademark of a distinctive double-bubble roof. It was this car, seen by Aston Martin's director Victor Gauntlett at the 1983 Geneva Motor Show, which led directly to the Aston Martin Zagato project.

Zagato started to go off the boil in the late 1980s. First it presented a vision of a future Aston Martin Lagonda called the Rapide, which was so poor that Aston Martin boss Victor Gauntlett took the unusual step of distancing his company from anything to do with it. Then came the Stelvio AZ1 project for

unmistakable trademark. By the 1970s, Zagato's importance had faded somewhat but its fortunes revived with the 1986 Aston Martin Zagato project, the Alfa Romeo SZ, Lancia Hyena, Nissan Autech Stelvio and series production of the Maserati Biturbo.

Zagato's self-financed dream cars have been relatively rare and rather inconsistent in their level of satisfaction. Alongside such sublime pieces as the Zeta 6, there have been some real disasters like the Stelvio and Lagonda Rapide. Zagato was forced to reform for the 1990s as SZ Design with Andrea Zagato at the helm.

Autech, a subdivision of Nissan. Unveiled in 1989, it was a two-plus-two coupé seemingly designed from the wing mirrors out (the front wings bulged out to accommodate them). Incredibly, it actually reached series production for the Japanese market. Zagato followed this exercise up with the more acceptable Gavia, Bambu and Seta projects, plus a Testarossa-based supercar called the Z93.

Perhaps marking a rebirth of the Zagato (or SZ Design) name was its 1996 Geneva showing and possible production model, the Raptor – its name recalling one of the villains of Steven Spielberg's dinosaur epic, *Jurassic Park*. Its proportions were exactly right, its Lamborghini Diablo V-twelve engine and four-wheel-drive system suitably exotic and its flop-forward double-

bubble canopy scintillating enough to engage the imagination. It justifies a link with the early, classic Zagato designs that make this *carrozzeria* a legend in car design.

■ ABOVE *For a powerful supercar, the Raptor succeeded in looking light and purposeful.*

■ BELOW *The Raptor revived Zagato's tradition of a prominent double-bubble roof. The car was based on Lamborghini parts.*

■ ABOVE *Zagato was effectively reborn in the 1990s. Its most promising project was the Raptor, developed for the 1996 Geneva Motor Show.*

■ OPPOSITE *The Hyena's hunched haunches gave a hint of high performance.*

I N D E X

LEFT: *Some people likened the oddball mS 1000 saloon (sedan) to a modern-day duo-tone Morris Minor. Certainly it reflected a trend towards "retro" design.*

PHOTOGRAPHIC CREDITS
The Publishers would like to thank the individual car manufacturers, The National Motor Museum at Beaulieu for the pictures on pages 9 top left and 38 top right, and *Classic and Sportscar* magazine, Haymarket Specialist Motoring, for supplying most of the pictures in the book.

BELOW: *The name Splash for this 1988 Ford concept car hinted at its capacity to get drenched without getting slushy carpets: the interior was waterproof!*